RAMBLE
AND REFRESH
ON THE
WELSH BORDERS

Twelve circular walks in the counties of Gwent, Powys,
Gloucestershire and Herefordshire featuring Tea Rooms

by

HEATHER AND JON HURLEY

Maps and line drawings by David Grech BA, B.Arch., RIBA

Published by
Thornhill Press
Cheltenham

MCMLXXXVIII

ISBN 0 946328 21 8

*Details given in this book are accurate at the time of writing;
neither the Publisher nor the Authors accept responsibility for
unforeseen alteration.*

Printed and bound by
Billing & Sons Limited, Worcester

CONTENTS

ACKNOWLEDGEMENTS

We wish to thank the following for their assistance: Hereford and Worcester County Council Engineering and Planning Department, Gwent County Council Planning Department and the Hereford City Library.

INTRODUCTION

Landscape

The southern Welsh Borders are beautiful and unspoilt with wooded hills, orchards, rich pastures and deep fertile valleys through which swift flowing rivers surge to their destination. From the heights of Hergest Ridge and the Great Doward to the low lying lands at Breinton and Leintwardine the rivers Wye, Clun, Usk, Monnow, Arrow and Teme provide delightful and timeless features in the counties of Gloucestershire, Gwent, Herefordshire and Powys. Fortunately much of the Wye Valley is carefully protected having been designated an Area of Outstanding Natural Beauty, a necessary move to preserve its landscape and wildlife.

History

From pre-historic times man has inhabited the Welsh Borders and left his mark on the landscape. Historical, industrial and architectural sites can be easily identified from the earliest Neolithic tomb at Dorstone, the wooded hill fort at Little Doward, the Roman road at Leintwardine and King Offa's Saxon dyke. The Normans defended their borders, constructing numerous castles, some of which can be seen and explored at Skenfrith, Crickhowell and Snodhill. Striking examples of period architecture too can be admired at 15th century Hergest Court and 18th century Berrington Hall. Even the industrial remains of the 19th century, like the man made ponds at Cannop and the disused railway tracks in the Forest of Dean add another interesting dimension to the overall scene.

Towns and Villages

Over the centuries market towns along the Welsh Borders, characterised now by their impressive clock towers, have evolved offering shopping, schooling, health and recreation in secure and cosy surroundings to the local inhabitants. The villages vary from the attractive and unspoilt Skenfrith to the more commercialised and scattered community at Symonds Yat. Another worthy feature of these border towns and villages is their ancient churches with their lofty towers and the more humble brick built chapels of the Victorian era.

5

Wildlife

Many of the areas covered by this book are sufficiently isolated to provide ideal habitats for our shyer species of animals and birds. During our walks we surprised a number of interesting creatures in terrain which included coverts from which cock pheasants raucously flashed, hedgerows hiding secretive snipe and flat fields where family groups of partridge timorously grazed. The indestructible pigeon, that bane of the farmer's life, was everywhere, great grey clouds of them swooping down like small aircraft to devour whole fields of sprouts. Plover were seen with their nodding punk hairdos, mewing and skipping at the merest sound of an intruder.

Along the rivers an eye was kept alert for the sly mink slipping into the water from trees up which they have been known to climb to sunbathe, or the less obvious otter living its quiet life beneath weirs and water falls. Herons rising out of foggy valleys screetching like miniature pterodactyl were a common sight, and swans, great white saintly processions of them gliding past. Tiny birds like mice flitting from alder to willow were constant delight and the common blackbird and thrush, leaving no one in doubt as to their skill, sang their hearts out atop swaying trees. In the loneliest parts of the countryside buzzards cried as they lumbered into the sky to whirl gracefully on the down draughts.

Rambles

The rambles for this guide have been chosen with the whole family in mind, offering varied scenery, interesting historical sites and outstanding views. Lesser known paths as well as clearly defined routes will lead walkers over hills, along riverbanks, through woodland and across farmland to pretty towns and villages where refreshments may be obtained. Four walks follow short stretches of the Wye Valley Walk, Offa's Dyke Path and Forest Trails all of which are waymarked. In one or two cases where there is an absence of signs the matter has been reported to the County Council, who are required by law to erect signposts at every point where a right of way joins a metalled road.

The rambles all follow definitive rights of way which are either footpaths, bridleways or public highways. If any problem is encountered it should be reported to the relevant County Council, Countryside Warden, Ramblers Association or local footpath group, whose addresses will be found at the back of this guide. It is worth noting that the description of the rambles may vary slightly according to seasonal changes and alterations to the landscape.

Equipment
It is advisable to carry the relevant Ordnance Survey Sheet, either 1:50,000 (1¼ inches to one mile) where rights of way are shown in red, or the 1:25,000 (2½ inches to one mile) series showing field boundaries and rights of way in green. When map reading remember to use churches, woods, rivers and buildings as landmarks to help confirm the route.

Other useful and necessary items should include sensible footwear, a lightweight waterproof and a comfortable rucksack to carry maps, compass, first aid and enough money to purchase refreshments.

Refreshments
Ramblers on the whole are a hardy and unfussy lot, who are quite content to sit overlooking some beautiful bit of countryside munching cheese, lettuce and brown bread sandwiches, and slurping from their flasks of decaffinated coffee. But for those who venture out on our circular walks, we have listed an excellent selection of tea shops, where for a few minutes they can wiggle their tired toes and enjoy the warmth, comfort and cleanliness of a good café.

The area in this guide boasts a surprisingly rich selection of tea shops where the cheerful owner's fare is well up to scratch. All the premises were nicely situated, most were well away from busy roads and they welcomed ramblers, their pets and children. It was noticeable that the health food movement was much in evidence and vegetarians were well treated too with a wide and interesting range of non meat dishes. The days of the ubiquitous pot of tea are gone and now one is spoilt for choice, with Indian, China and other scented delights to choose from. 'Home made' was the key phrase everywhere, ranging from delicate crispy biscuits to great chunks of flab inducing fruit cake.

Certain tea shops are closed for part of the year so a few good pubs have been included. No doubt some ramblers who would not be seen dead in a tea shop would prefer to sip real ale in front of a log fire. Just a couple of minor recurring points, please remove muddy boots and do not produce your own flask and sandwiches on the premises. Remember tea shops and pubs sometimes struggle to make a living. Spare a thought and purchase your refreshments from them, it keeps them going.

THE COUNTRY CODE

Enjoy the countryside and respect its life and work.
Guard against all risk of fire.
Fasten all gates.
Keep your dogs under close control.
Keep to public paths across farmland.
Use gates and stiles to cross fences, hedges and walls.
Leave livestock, crops and machinery alone.
Take your litter home.
Help to keep all water clean.
Protect wildlife, plants and trees.
Take special care on country roads.
Make no unnecessary noise.

Cemetery Gateway, Leintwardine.

1. LEINTWARDINE ROAD

4 miles

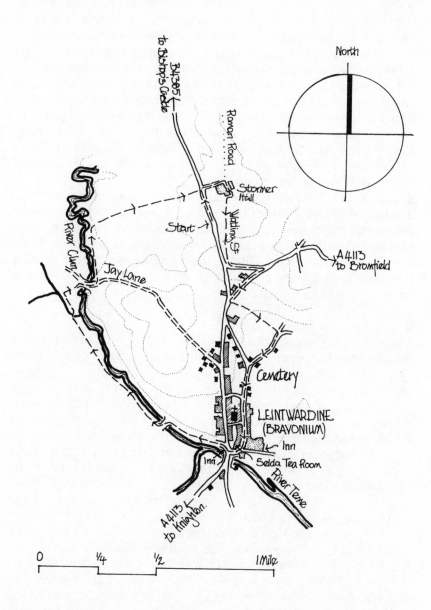

One of the most important roads the Romans built was Watling Street, which was probably constructed by Governor Frontinus during the early part of the first century. It ran from Dover to Wroxeter, and remains can still be seen at Leintwardine in Herefordshire where it joins the neighbouring border county of Shropshire. This attractive village has grown and developed within the old fortifications of a Roman Camp called Bravonium, where defensive banks and the course of Watling Street are still visible.

Leintwardine is full of interest; its buildings, of various styles and ages, line the parallel streets surrounding the elevated church of St. Mary Magdalene. On the south side the river Clun joins the Teme crossed here by a handsome stone bridge built in the early 19th century and widened in 1930. Views of the hills of South Shropshire, Mocktree and the Wigmore Rolls can be enjoyed during this four mile ramble.

This route follows the remains of the Roman Road from Stormer Hall to Leintwardine, when a leisurly stroll through the village halts for some excellent refreshments at Selda tea shop. Beside the bridge a well defined path along the banks of the Teme leads to the meandering Clun as far as Jay Lane, where another Roman site has been discovered. Wide level pastures make a pleasant return to the car.

Route

Cars can be parked at a small lay by (GR 402753) on the B4385 near the entrance to Stormer Hall, about one mile north of Leintwardine. From here walk north along the road, then turn right to follow a farm track also serving as the right of way leading to the left hand side of rambling farm buildings at Stormer Hall. Between a large oak and a wayside pond runs the course of the Roman Road, but as the farm has been built across the ancient route, the present path goes right between high outbuildings, then sharp right again through the yard. At the gate bear left returning to the line of the Roman route easily identified by the sparce and stunted hawthorn hedge. This is followed through fields till reaching a large overhanging ash tree, where a wire fence is crossed. Walk diagonally right across the sloping meadow with fine views all around of distant hills and valleys, so typical of this borderland. Opposite a red brick cottage, cross an iron hurdle leading onto the road.

Turn left along the quiet road lined with an interesting and varied hedgerow of holly, maple, elder, hawthorn, blackberry, dog rose and crab apple where, as we passed, a pair of finches were

12

singing joyfully in the late summer sun. At the junction follow the busier road to the right descending past Hightree house, Cottage and Petrol Station, also Leintwardine Manor which is undergoing conversion into more prosaic flats. At the next road junction turn sharply left to follow an undefined footpath over a gate under a splendid ash, across an L-shaped field to a stile, then straight ahead through the next field to a gate leading onto a metalled lane.

Follow this lane to the right, which soon passes between the high stone walls of the former vicarage and pink washed cottages. Now in the village of Leintwardine the way continues to the left along Watling Street past modern school buildings and a cemetery with an unusual entrance dated 1901. This street has a crowded mixture of cottages, barns, shops and houses either stone or timber framed, some beautifully restored while others remain derelict. A right turn leads to the 900 year old church with its massive tower.

The pleasant churchyard is hemmed in by houses which overlook weathered tombs, and a convenient seat is shaded by a graceful silver birch. The church's dark interior features two side chapels, the scanty remains of a 15th century reredos and nicely carved choir stalls which probably came from Wigmore Abbey after the Dissolution of the Monastries. A novelty is the internal mechanism of a disused clock, one of the oldest of its type, dating from the 16th century. Originally in the tower the clock is now displayed near the porch. Having explored the church, retrace your steps back to Watling Street which shortly reaches Selda, a tea and coffee house attractively situated beside the village green overlooking the river Teme.

Refreshment
Selda is a well managed tea shop with a history extending back to 1612. Amid nice old fashioned items of furniture, in a whitewashed and beamed room, the walker can be sure his or her well being is in careful hands. The owner still believes in fresh food and lightly cooked, or indeed crunchingly raw vegetables to keep the rambler's teeth as well as his tummy in good fettle. It is a pleasantly relaxing setting with around the walls pictures by local artists which are for sale. Part of the floor is still stone flagged, a gas bottle comfortingly burbles with contentment and a sign prohibits both dogs and smokers.

The menu is novel with at least three different kinds of tea, Darjeeling, Lapsang and Earl Grey. There are plenty of other drinks to choose from including coffee, soft drinks and the unusual Hot Milk with Nutmeg. Cakes and jams are homemade as are the soups and snacks, and the claim on the menu to provide 'varied food to nourish and please' is not a vain one. Fresh sandwiches are always available with several choices of filling, and we were rather taken by the Ham and Peanut Butter combination.

Through the windows the green banks of the Teme may be espied, loftily shaded by a giant chestnut under which local children gambol in the midday sun. The premises also house a gift shop which sells books, cards, chunky woollen garments, pottery, Welsh crafts and quality cosmetics. Indecently bulging with Parsnip and Tomato Bake and Cheese Puff we happily waddled along on the second half of this most attractive and enjoyable ramble.

Selda is open all year round, but is closed on Sundays and Mondays from November to the end of February. There are a number of varied alternatives for refreshments in the village.

The Sun Inn romantically rustic where a good refreshing pint may be had in quite nostalgic comfort.

The Lion Hotel across the road can supply meals as well as a selection of beers, wines and soft drinks.

The Fiddler's Elbow where fish and chips sizzle deliciously and provide a mouthwatering car or picnic snack.

Return

From the tea shop, cross the road and walk along the riverside to admire the attractive stone bridge spanning the Teme above a forceful weir. Keeping right of the bridge pass the Lion Hotel and a garage, then turn left along Mill Lane, where the only footpath sign seen on this route directs walkers along a pleasant byway. Behind cottages and former mills the Teme is joined by the Clun, and it is this river that the right of way follows. Climb the gate ahead and shortly turn left to cross a wooden bridge over the Clun. Now turn right and follow the banks of this dark, and in places quite deep river, where its banks are a favourite haunt for trout fishermen.

The low lying meadows are grazed by fawn coloured Charolais and the more common black and white Fresians who appeared unconcerned as we rambled through their pastures. Stiles lead away from the river to a footbridge across a brook, and the farm buildings at Jay can be seen. The path continues ahead keeping the brook on the left and at another footbridge turn sharp right across the large field to rejoin the banks of the Clun. Here in the autumn sun huge inquisitive heavy horses with their young eagerly gallop in the golden stubble.

14

A more substantial road bridge crosses the Clun at Jay Lane, but leave the lane immediately by turning left over a hurdle to follow the footpath along the eastern bank of the river. Standing as sentinels, strange concrete blocks form part of a water system. Just south of here is the site of a Roman marching camp. Another long broad field is traversed, in which handsome white faced Herefords grazed contentedly amongst hundreds of sheep cropping the sweet grass under trees of mistletoe. Before the tapering end of this meadow, where the Clun meanders sharply to the left, don't miss the line of the right of way which goes in the opposite direction over a low fence. This missing stile has been reported to the County Council. Continue straight ahead where a succession of gates lead through level pastures to the road opposite the path to Stormer Hall.

The Clock Tower, Knighton.

2 KNIGHTON TOWN
2½ miles

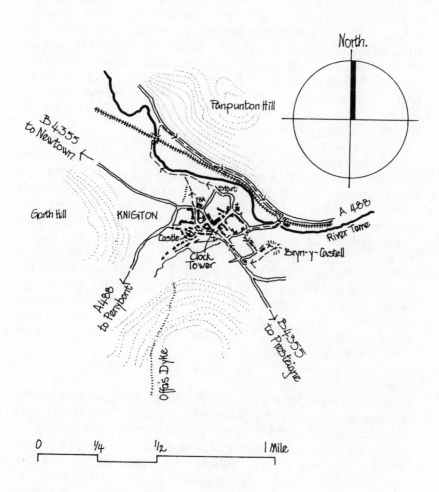

North.

Panpunton Hill

B 4355 to Newtown ←

Garth Hill

KNIGTON

start

YHA

Castle

Clock Tower

A488 to Penybont ←

A 488

River Teme

Bryn-y-Castell

Offa's Dyke

B 4355 to Presteigne ↘

0   ¼   ½   1 Mile

17

Below the great hill of Panpunton and the conifer clad slopes of Kinsley Wood lies the market town of Knighton, sheltered in the valley of the Teme. Small and friendly it is now firmly established in the county of Powys in Wales; before the Act of Union in 1536 it was in England, deriving its name from the English 'Knights' Town'. The Welsh Tref-y-Clawdd means 'Town of the Dyke', and it is with this linear earthwork of Offa's that archeologists, historians and walkers associate the town.

King Offa ruled Mercia in the 8th century and laboriously constructed his amazing dyke to form a boundary between Mercia and Wales. Extensive remains have survived, and a good local stretch can be admired at Pinner's Hole in Knighton. In 1971 the Offa's Dyke Path was opened; from Chepstow to Prestatyn it closely follows the Welsh Borders and the line of the Dyke through glorious unspoilt countryside.

On a pleasant day this easy stroll is rather short, but it is very suitable for the elderly, less active and young children. For the more energetic a steep climb up Panpunton Hill reaching 1200 feet may be an attractive alternative difficult to resist. From Knighton's riverside car park the walk follows a short section of the waymarked long distance path along the banks of the unpolluted leafy shallows of the river Teme. Having crossed the county boundary, a quiet Shropshire lane winds below the steep wooded slopes of Kinsley Wood to Knighton. The town is an appealing mixture comprising a restored Norman church, several chapels, an ancient market, a modern Community Centre, two castle sites, the interesting Offa's Dyke Centre, a 19th century railway, varied shops and old inns with the Victorian clock tower, a typical border town feature, as its epicentre.

Route
Knighton's riverside car park (GR 287727) is the starting point for this short stroll. Follow the waymarked route of Offa's Dyke Path through the gate alongside the swift waters of the Teme flowing below the coniferous slopes of Panpunton Hill and Kinsley Wood. This side, the river bank is covered with traditional trees of ash, hazel and beech where rooks, jackdaws and larks fly high in the valley. A modest and unobtrusive picnic site overlooks the river, a most delightful setting where gates lead to an open stretch. On a hot summer's day it is hard to resist a paddle in this crystal clear mountain water. Along here are splendid views of the surrounding hills and the bird life continues to be interesting, dippers flash

above the fresh water and jet black crows irritably flap their wings at being disturbed.

The waymarked path crosses the river beside an iron railway bridge built in 1861 which still carries the line connecting Swansea to Shrewsbury. A sharp left turn leads across the railway track and the route continues along the opposite bank of the Teme lined with crowded alders. Almost regretfully the path leaves the river and gently ascends to meet a metalled lane. Here the more active can start the steep climb up Panpunton Hill by following Offa's Dyke Path, but our more sedate route turns right along the lane.

After passing a nicely kept farm and a house at Lower Panpunton, Knighton church tower comes into view. A high fence along the railway hides the town, but the outskirts are soon reached. Rows of brick, stone and whitewashed cottages with thriving vegetable plots stand opposite the thick woods of Kinsley, managed by the Forestry Commission. A short flight of steps lead invitingly into the woods where beech trees shade the overgrown quarries. See if you can spot the miniature mural of a silhouetted street scene painted on the bare cottage wall.

By a tall and interesting building called Kinsley House turn right along the main road across the boundary from Shropshire into Wales. The railway track is crossed by a brick bridge and the river by a more attractive stone structure above a fierce weir. Below, as we crossed, a team of men thigh deep in icy water were working with large machines reinforcing the banks of the Teme. Bear right into the town along Station Road where a variety of small shops and cottages line the street. At a gap on the right St. Edwards church with its short squat tower can be seen at the end of Church Road.

Turn left along Bowling Green Lane where on market days the baying and roaring of livestock cannot be ignored amidst a busy typically rural gathering of farmers, autioneers and onlookers. At the attractive modern Community Centre turn left through a gate into a children's playground, then climb one of the slippery paths to the top of Bryn-y-Castell. Here an elevated view of the town with its working mills, football and cricket pitches, market and Community Centre intermingled with red brick houses all protected by wooden hills, may be savoured. Descend the mound and take the footpath behind the centre and tennis courts which joins a paved path with iron railings. This leads to Broad Street.

This main street is followed to the right passing a rich amalgam of shops, banks and inns before reaching the clock tower standing prominently on the site of the old town hall. This monument was presented to the town by Thomas Moore Esq. in 1872, and its chimes provide an appealing background as one enters the Clock Tower Tea Shop.

Refreshment
The Clock Tower Tea Shop fits snugly into a corner of a large ironmongers, looking out onto the Victorian edifice which gives Knighton much of its old market town character. Tastefully decorated in stone and wood with a large sealed stone fireplace as an interesting feature, the tea room is comfortable, clean and admirably hospitable. There is an adequate menu offering a variety of tasty items which includes snacks, salads, soups, cakes and cream teas. The soup was admittedly not of the home made kind the day we called, but we were cheerfully assured it usually is.

A bowl of soup and a hot Toastie is usually enough for the starving walker, but a slice of quiche is not to be sneezed at either, especially when it is appetisingly made and served steaming hot. As well as a range of toasted sandwiches there were jacket potatoes with a number of different fillings, curry, ham, cheese and pineapple. Salads were all accompanied with thick slices of bread still warm from the nearby bakery. For afters there was a selection of pastries and buns. We enjoyed a slab of rich fruit cake which arrived buttered! It went beautifully with the strong freshly made Cona coffee. Tea and soft drinks were to hand and the service was cheerful and welcoming.

The store itself stocks a wide array of household goods ranging from Rayburn stoves to hedge cutter mittens, bone china and cut glass. Adjacent to the tea room there is a well stocked peas and pulses department, where displayed in open necked sacks is a fine collection of eatables, from black eyed beans to long grain rice, barley, raisins and in fact everything for the whole foodie and vegetarian. No problem, either, with opening times, the Clock Tower Tea Shop opens normal hours, except Sundays, and happily there are several alternatives.

Browns a bakery up the Narrows, a tilted street by the Clock Tower. Here refreshments may be enjoyed with an added advantage, the bread is straight from the oven.

George and Dragon offers something a bit more potent. An old inn built in 1637, and very adjacent to the centre of the town.

Norton Arms is a large rambling hotel with the usual fare associated with such a place.

Return

After the hospitality of the tea room cross Broad Street to the steep High Street also known as the Narrows, which winds around an ancient castle site concealed by antique and craft shops. At the top turn right passing the Baptist Chapel founded in 1865.

Ahead stands the old primary school, now housing a Youth Hostel and the Offa's Dyke Heritage Centre, open every day in the summer except Sundays, but unfortunately closed during the winter months. Inside one can learn all about King Offa and the construction of his Dyke from the detailed exhibition. There is also a good selection of literature for sale together with maps, tourist board leaflets and a number of sourvenirs.

From the Heritage Centre follow Offa's Dyke Path across a picnic and play ground forming the riverside park which was completed through the generosity of a local man, William Hadfield, who is commenorated by a chunky memorial stone below the drooping branches of a silver birch. A section of the dyke can be investigated before a rustic sign directs the way to stone steps leading back to the banks of the river Teme. Here a right turn takes the walker back to the car park.

Eye Church & Manor.

Berrington Hall.

3   BERRINGTON PARK

7 miles

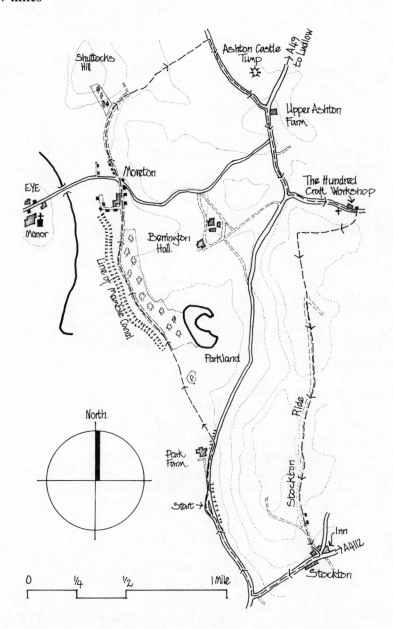

In the wonderful open countryside of north Herefordshire, with far reaching views of the Black Mountains, Radnor Forest, Croft Ambrey and Bircher Common, lies the beautiful parkland encompassing the impressive building of Berrington Hall. Thomas Harley purchased this estate in the 1770s when he built the house designed by Holland. The extensive park contains a 14 acre lake, various plantations, a pheasantry and gardens landscaped by the brilliant Capability Brown. The whole estate is surrounded by a decaying wrought iron fence, parts of which are now being restored. The National Trust acquired the property in 1957 so the lavishly decorated house with its interesting range of outbuildings are now open to the public on certain days during the summer, and a good tea is served in the Servants' Hall.

Berrington Hall is situated in the parish of Eye, where another important house, Eye Manor, can be seen. Also owned by Thomas Harley, the manor built of mellow brick in 1680 stands in a commanding position together with its 12th century church overlooking Berrington Park. Another historical feature in this parish are the scanty remains of the Mamble Canal, an 18th century waterway constructed to connect Kington, Leominster and Stourbridge, but only the Leominster to Mamble section was completed, enabling coal to be transported to Leominster.

This energetic ramble of seven miles comprises field, road and woodland walking, although in winter parts of the route can be very muddy. Two short stretches along the main road are compensated by the bracing exposed views of this borderland country, the varied woods and a fine mixture of pastures, which for the more active is a rewarding experience.

From its start near Kimbolton the walk stays close to the great boundary of the Berrington estate, where it is interesting and sad to see how time erodes all traces of even the noblest of dynasties. At Moreton field paths lead to the tea room and craft workshop at Lower Hundred, and a lengthy stretch along the Stockton Ride brings one to the small cosy inn at Stockton Cross. All in all a fairly demanding walk which will extend even the more experienced of ramblers.

Route

Cars can be safely parked at the lay-by (GR 510615) on the Leominster to Ludlow main road. Walk north along the wide grass verge for about 500 yards, then after passing Park Farm enter the first field gate on the left at the bottom of the road embankment. This is the start of a seldom used bridle-way which diagonally

24

crosses the field to a gate in the right hand corner. Once in this large meadow bear right between the lone oak on the left and a small coppice to the right. At this point walk alongside the wrought iron boundary fence, which encircles Berrington Hall and Park, until reaching Moreton.

A red brick Keeper's Cottage shortly comes into view, virtually hidden behind trees and the boundary fence. To its left the woods forming part of Moreton Ride are reached by a gate and a plank bridge across a brook, then a stile. The path becomes more clearly defined as it leaves the woods to follow through open fields. Here traces of the Mamble Canal are visible on the left. The next gate leads onto an enclosed track where the elegant Eye Manor with its church can be clearly seen. The boundary fence disappears as one approaches the farm and the barns and cottages at Moreton.

Continue straight across the tarmac lane where the bridleway serves several pretty cottages. Between arable fields the path skirts a dark conifer wood called Shuttocks Plantations. Sandstone from its old quarries were used to build Berrington Hall, and a special tramway was apparently constructed to transport stone to Berrington. Where the track veers sharply left continue ahead along the line of the footpath keeping to the left hand hedge. These fields are dotted with mature oaks which attract pairs of flashing finches, magpies, dunnocks, crows, colourful tits and squalking jays. Later we spied a rasping corncrake and a hen pheasant darting along in the sun.

At the end of the field bear right and cross a brook, but continue in the same direction keeping the hedge to the left. The ground rises passing a field full of currant bushes before reaching a tarmaced lane followed to the right. A fishing pool glints in the sun below Ashton Castle Tump, a motte and bailey on the edge of a spur. High hop trellises on the right remind us the hop kilns coming into view at Upper Ashton Farm will be in use again next year.

The main road is re-joined which is followed to the right. An iron milepost, a bygone of the turnpike age, informs us that we are but four miles from Leominster and seven from Ludlow. This busy thoroughfare twists and turns through Ashton with its farms and cottages offering fresh fruit, organically produced potatoes, goat's milk, free range eggs and holiday accommodation. At the brow of the hill we gratefully leave the road by turning left along Hundred Lane, a more peaceful byway, signed 'The Hundred'. A tiny tin chapel with its graveyard is passed on the right just before arriving at our refreshment stop.

Refreshment

The Lower Hundred Craft Workshop and Tea Room is an attractive stone barn at the back of a red bricked cottage. It has been tastefully renovated and converted into a comfortable tearoom with a wide range of crafts on display. The three tables at one end cater for the thirsty shoppers and the menu, though tiny, is sufficient to knock the edge off the famished rambler's appetite. It consists mainly of cakes and biscuits which I was assured are all homemade. The craftshop is crammed with paintings, pictures, pottery stone rabbits, cards, booklets and a large collection of homemade candles of various shapes and sizes. There is also plenty of information available for the car bound visitor including a useful map of the surrounding villages and towns listing sights of historical interest. Times of opening are from April to November. The only alternative refreshment place is near the end of the ramble at Kimbolton.

The Stockton Cross Inn is open all the year round, an advantage the pub has over the opposition. This small inn is very ordinary with formica topped furniture, quoits, darts and a woodburning stove. Only crisps, freshly filled rolls, chocolate bars and well kept ale are available here. A few elderly men exchanged gossip in the time honoured way as their forefathers did, except today they have to compete with a huge colour television set blasting away unwatched over their heads. Still, pubs like 'The Cross' are a welcome sight when the tea shops operate part-time.

Return

Leaving the craft workshop the way continues left along the lane for about 150 yards, then take a right turn opposite the thatched 'Hundred Cottage'. Cross a stile supported by a large tree stump, walk straight across the small orchard to a gate and turn right here through a broad meadow to another stile. Keep the hedge to the right and continue to the top of the hill where a magnificent scene across to Ludlow and the Shropshire hills can be fully appreciated.

A sharp left turn, this side of the gate, leads along a lengthy footpath leading through fields alongside a narrow strip of woodland called Stockton Ride. Upon reaching this wood and having passed Hawthorn Farm 300 yards away in the eastern valley, the path at present has to be abandoned due to a number of obstructions. An acceptable alternative is to turn right and enter Stockton Ride where a well defined track leads in the same direction for nearly one mile. If in the meantime the County Council have carried out the necessary improvements then the field

26

path can be followed instead. Where the wood finishes bear left along a gravel drive to the road and the Stockton Cross Inn.

After a refreshing drink turn right along the road to join the Leominster to Ludlow main road again. Follow it to the right passing a barn with unusual blocked windows. A wide grass verge leads safely back to your starting point.

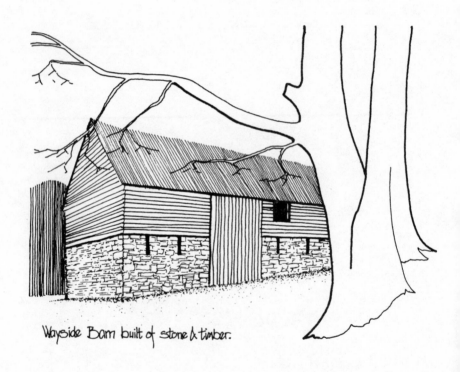

Wayside Barn built of stone & timber.

4   LOWER HERGEST
6 miles

OS Sheet 148

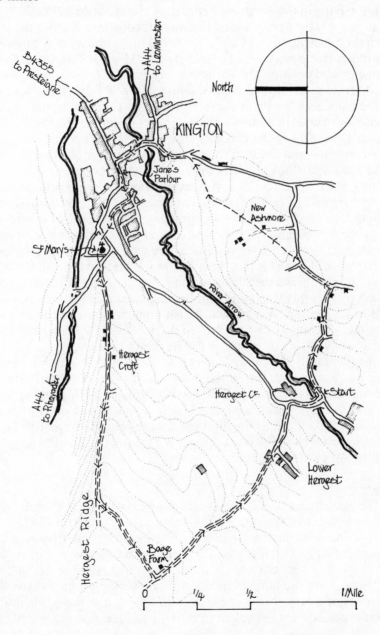

North

B4355 to Presteigne

↑A44 to Leominster

KINGTON

Jane's Parlour

New Ashmore

St Mary's

River Arrow

A44 to Rhayader

Hergest Croft

Hergest Ct.

★Start

Lower Hergest

Hergest Ridge

Badge Farm

0   ¼   ½   1 Mile

Lower Hergest is a tiny hamlet sheltered by the windswept slopes of Hergest Ridge, famous for its extensive and picturesque views of the Welsh Borders. It is only two miles from the market town of Kington lying in the north west corner of Herefordshire. For such a small place Hergest has a long and well documented history dating from the construction of Castle Twts. All that remains of the motte and bailey is a green mound overlooked by Hergest Court standing in an elevated position above the rushing waters of the river Arrow. A stone and partly timber framed house, Hergest Court was the seat of the Vaughan family in the 15th century. Tales of mystery and legend surround the family and the house, including the story of a hound appearing as the ghost of Black Vaughan. The spectre was duly exorcised and reduced to such minute proportions that it was locked in a snuff box and thrown into Hergest Pool.

Hergest itself is associated with several literary figures, the earliest being, a friend of Chaucer's, Sir John Clanvowe 1341−91 who wrote a poem 'The Cuckoo and the Nightingale'. Lewis Glyn Cothi, one of the greatest Welsh Bards of the 15th century was connected with the Vaughans; he wrote an elegy on Black Vaughan which gives a detailed description of Hergest at that time. At a much later date Arthur Conan Doyle stayed at Hergest Croft when he wrote 'The Hound of the Baskervilles', and this popular tale bears some similarity to the legend of Black Vaughan. A medieval Welsh manuscript acquired by the Vaughans became known as the Red Book of Hergest because of the colour of its covers. It is now in the Bodleian Library.

Our pleasantly hilly hike leads from Hergest Bridge along quiet winding lanes and forgotten field paths to Kington. Here refreshments may be enjoyed together with a quick tour of the town's market, museum and church before following a short stretch of Offa's Dyke Path to the high open moorland of Hergest Ridge. From here a well defined track steeply descends to Lower Hergest and the valley of the Arrow.

Route

At Hergest Bridge (GR 280551) cars can be parked in the small lay-by beside the swift flowing Arrow. In an easterly direction follow a narrow metalled lane past prettily sited cottages at Breadward. From here we had planned to take a right of way across fields to the banks of the river, but the footpath was inaccessible so one must continue along the lane. Notice a wayside spring gushing through the roots of a large ash tree before climbing to the top of the hill, where tremendous views of Bradnor Hill and Hergest Ridge can be savoured. We also enjoyed watching an assortment of hens scratching and pecking under the wintry fruit bushes at Bramble Cottage, where hedgerows still glinted with autumnal yellows and golds under a watery sun.

At the junction bear left around a neat stone and timber barn sheltered by old and gnarled beeches providing a picturesque scene overlooking a valley of sloping patchwork fields so typical of Herefordshire. Soon a tall radio mast reminds us that we are of the 20th century. Turn left opposite a small coppice of hazel, birch, beech and oak to follow an undefined footpath to Kington. The stile by the holly tree is at present overgrown so continue along the lane till reaching the field gate. Once in the field walk back to the holly tree and carefully follow the path as described.

Walk diagonally right across the field to a stile, then diagonally again across the next field to the left of the farm and buildings at New Ashmore. Here keep right of the corner gate and cross a rustic stile to the left of a timber barn. Within a few yards an almost hidden stile leads back into open farmland. Continue diagonally to a line of trees on the left, where a wire fence is crossed (another stile missing) beside an ash. The line is followed ahead through wide pastures to a gate standing to the right of a row of oak trees in the hedge. From here Kington can be clearly seen above the silos standing like an obsolete space station adjoining the more traditional scene of grazing cattle and ponies. The church dominates the town's buildings of stone and red brick, and the bracken clad slopes of Bradnor Hill scarred with sheep tracks provides a backcloth as the hidden Arrow winds its way through the town.

From this gate turn right, where the path follows a line of remaining tree stumps, before bearing left to the corner field gate leading onto the road opposite a house called Redlands. Follow this road to the left and Kington is soon reached after passing a clump of derelict farm buildings. On the outskirts a former octagonal toll house has been sympathetically restored and extended, and nearby antique furniture restorations can be viewed in a workshop. The busy Arrow is crossed by an undistinguished bridge by the delicensed Old Bridge Inn. Beside a quieter mill race a tall mill serves as a corn merchants. Along Bridge Street churches and chapels of all faiths were represented together with art and antique shops. On meeting High Street turn left where the comfort of Jane's Parlour will be found at the rear of a baker's shop.

Refreshments

Jane's Parlour, slap in the middle of town, has plenty to offer the ravenous rambler. The tea room at the back of a bread shop is black and white with painted beams and blue plates on racks. Heating is by convector, but it is small and comfortable with seating for two dozen souls. The menu is vast, offering almost everything from plain bacon and eggs to a variety of quiches, baked potatoes with a selection of at least six fillings, curry and rice, sandwiches, lasagne, cold meats, cod and chips plus a selection of sweets, cakes and ices. Service is brisk and smiling, and the owner Derek Wood is a chatty and humorous man whose book 'Maggots Green' was due out in 1987. Illustrated by border artist Robert Palmer it is based on local happenings.

Drinks of a non alcoholic nature include good dark Kenco coffee, pots of tea and pop for the kids, who also have quite an appealing menu all to themselves, full of such things as fish fingers, the sort of food the little angels crave at home but never get. The shop sells fresh Radnorshire bread and cakes, and also stocks soft drinks, crisps, Cornish pasties and pork pies. Jane's parlour is open every day of the week except Sundays.

There are a number of alternative eating places on both sides of this busy street so finding a suitable place to have one's break presents no problems.

Queen's Head is an interesting convivial Whitbread pub where snacks may be obtained.

Fish Bar and Restaurant for a tasty snack.

The Burton Hotel built in 1851.

Return

From Jane's Parlour continue along High Street, with its old fashioned shops and interesting alley ways, till reaching the red brick market hall built by Kempson in 1885 to replace an earlier 17th century building by John Abel. The regulation border town clock tower was added in the jubilee year of 1897. Follow Mill Street passing the recently opened Kington Museum where agricultural, industrial and household implements of the past are displayed. Just beyond the primary school turn right up Churchill Road, and before the fire station take a left turn through a swing gate. A narrow footpath leads behind fertile gardens and bears right along a pleasant secluded stretch to reach the road immediately opposite Kington church.

St. Marys church appears as a three tiered construction with an

St. Marys church appears as a three tiered construction with an almost detached tower dating from the 13th century. It stands in a large graveyard with remarkedly few tombstones. Inside the dark building one's eye is caught by the striking stained glass of the east window. Apart from the monument to Thomas Vaughan and his wife of the 1460s, another memorial to John Morris attracted our attention. It commemorates a Kington man who died at the age of 72 in 1833 who left £10,000 to the Hereford Infirmary which was opened in 1783. Morris is described as an 'able, warm and zealous friend'.

Leave the churchyard by Wyche House, and keep straight ahead, cross the main road and follow Offa's Dyke Path signed to Ridgebourne and Hergest Croft. Houses of this name built at the turn of the century are passed together with the attractive gardens at Hergest Croft, where visitors enjoy spectacular views of blooming rhododendrons and azaleas in May and June. For about a further mile the path rises towards the bracken covered hill of Hergest Ridge, which is reached by a gate. Keep to a left hand track which serves as a bridleway, and what a delight it must be to canter a willing horse across these grassy slopes.

From Hergest Ridge far reaching views of the Radnorshire hills can be fully appreciated, while to the south the gentler Herefordshire landscape can be admired. The path leaves the ridge bearing left along a windswept boundary hedge of holly, beech and thorn growing alongside the scanty remains of an ancient stone wall. Before the farm at Bage a healthy herd of cattle grazed, carefully guarded by an enormous Charolais bull.

At the fir coppice beside the farm turn sharply left, where the right of way descends past Bage Farm along a gravel track. A rushing brook rising from the copious springs on the hillside keeps the walker company, before a gate and cattle grid lead to a metalled lane steeply descending to Lower Hergest. At the minor road junction a mound on the left is all that remains of Castle Twts. Keep ahead following the lane to the next junction opposite the mysterious Hergest Court with its long history of tales and legends. Here turn right and around a bend where Hergest Bridge will be seen.

Whitney Bridge

5   WHITNEY WOOD

5 miles

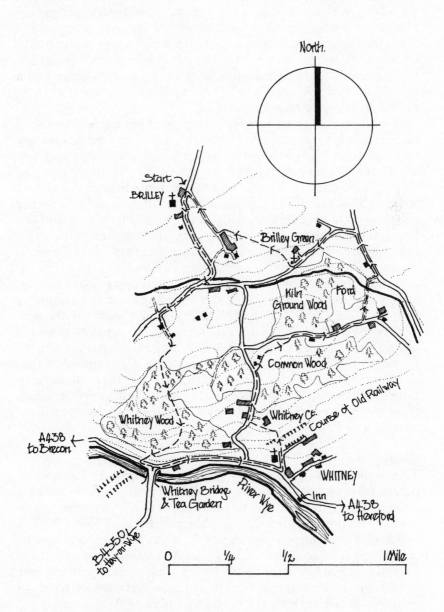

The small riverside village of Whitney lies on the edge of the Wye's flood plain, below the neighbouring parish of Brilley and the Welsh boundary. Steep wooded hills, so typical of the Wye Valley, rise above Whitney's 18th century church, toll bridge, tea garden and pleasant inn. Whitney Wood covers the western slopes, where a mixed woodland has been recently cleared leaving mature oaks standing above a matted carpet of bracken and brambles. Uncharacteristic rhododendrons grow on the lower slopes, and a variety of bird life enjoys the privacy of these woods including pheasants, tits and tree creepers.

Whitney is only four miles from Hay-on-Wye now famous for its second hand book shops. This market town can be reached by crossing an unusual toll bridge, which has an interesting and well documented history dating from the days of a former ford replaced by a stone bridge in 1773. The strong and unpredictable currents of the river Wye caused the first three bridges to collapse, so a timber and stone structure was specially designed and built to withstand heavy floods. Since 1802 it has survived the vagaries of the river, sun, snow, frost and rain and the transition from horse drawn to motor driven vehicles.

In this unknown but beautiful walking area, we discovered an interesting and varied five mile route leading from the heights of Brilley. Quiet lanes and rutted tracks steeply descend through Whitney Woods. At the toll bridge refreshments are only available during the summer months, but an excellent alternative can be found at the Boat Inn. Whitney church can be viewed before returning up the hilly slope, where well defined paths twist and turn through Common Wood and Kiln Ground Wood. A gentler climb from the isolated hamlet at Brilley Green leads across open fields and back to Brilley church.

Route
This walk starts from Brilley church (GR 261493) standing at nearly 600 feet above the Wye Valley. There is ample parking between the church and the old school built in 1808 by John Harris who is commemorated in St. Marys church. This building underwent restoration at the end of the 19th century only to lose its tower and roof in a fire of 1910, so the unusual tower with its pyramid roof dates back to this event. Follow the metalled lane descending in a southerly direction bearing left across a hidden unnamed brook rushing ahead to join the river Wye.

The lane rises, but before the brow of the hill turn left through a

36

gate and over a cattle grid, where the right of way passes between two cottages to a stile. Ahead the enclosed track soon reaches another gate leading into a sheltered field. Here turn sharply right, through the field and cross the corner stile into Whitney Wood. The path is unclear at first, part of the woodland having been recently felled, but it winds diagonally through undergrowth to the hilltop, where a defined and sunken track steeply descends down a muddy and rutted slope.

Glimpses of the Wye will soon be spied through an unusual thicket of rhododendrons and holly. This is where the path veers right running parallel above the river and the disused railway track, to arrive at the main road nearly opposite Whitney Bridge and Toll House where refreshments are obtainable during the summer. Before stopping walk past the toll house dated 1797, through the modern toll gate past an old pump and across the stone and timber bridge to admire the views of the riverside, a dismantled railway bridge, the thick woods of Whitney, Merbach Hill and the neverending Welsh hills beyond Hay-on-Wye. Below, pigeons nest in the framework unperturbed by disturbances, and even the odd cormorant can be seen flying high above the Wye.

Refreshment

At the Whitney Bridge Tea Garden the placid Wye flows serenely past as the walker sits in the sun devouring his food with a cup of strong tea. That's the theory, but in winter the river swells and causes alarm as it creeps up and over its banks and floods wide areas of green pastures. Whole trees wedge themselves against the toll bridge piers, and enough flotsam and jetsam is left by the receding flood to feed a wood burner all winter. Let us assume that it is a spring or summer day when to sit by the river must be divine. The wooden seats and tables don't look their best off season, but a lick of paint and a scythe through the rough couch grass should make the Toll House Tea Garden more than adequate.

A small kitchen copes, I am told, with plenty of orders for soups, toasted sandwiches, quiches, salads and sundry sticky buns and scones. As well as tea and coffee, a fair variety of soft drinks is sold. A small kiosk dispenses ice creams, lollies and also stocks Germolene and sticking plasters, not a bad idea if you are a walker. Being on the main Hereford to Brecon road the Tea Garden does a brisk trade in early morning breakfasts, and many a hungry traveller has been known to pull in for an early egg, bacon and banger by the riverside. More normal opening times are from 10 a.m. to 6 p.m. from Easter to the end of September. An alternative eating place is within half a mile.

The Boat Inn at Whitney where we enjoyed a very pleasant lunch at this well appointed and comfortable pub. Splendid views of the Wye can be obtained from spacious picture windows, and a log fire spluttered and sparked. The menu is above Herefordshire pub norms and a wine list offers a few nice bottles of vino.

Return

From the bridge follow the main road towards Hereford, where the wide grass verge provides a safe walkway. The milestone dates back to the days when this was a turnpike road during the 18th and 19th centuries. A toll was paid for the privilege of travelling along these routes which were improved and maintained by the appointed Turnpike Trustees. Iron railings enclose riverside meadows and a red brick pumphouse which once supplied water to Whitney Court.

The Boat Inn is within half a mile of the tea garden, tucked away overlooking the river Wye, but if not required follow the second turning on the left leading to Whitney church which is dedicated to St. Peter and St. Paul. Built in 1740 it replaced an earlier building destroyed by floods in 1735. Some of the original materials were re-used, including the 13th century font. An attractive and unusual feature is the carved wooden war memorial in a blocked doorway. From the churchyard gate turn left along the lane to a swing gate ahead which leads to a collapsed railway footbridge.

The Hereford, Hay and Brecon Railway opened in 1864 and continued in use until 1962 when the track was dismantled. Unfortunately this footbridge, forming a public right of way, has been neglected. While the local councils and British Rail are attempting to re-instate it, it is necessary to scramble carefully down and up the deep cutting. At the other side bear left following the well trodden path leading between open fields and Whitney Court, built of stone by the Watsons at the turn of the century. There are fine views of the meandering Wye before reaching the swing gate leading to a metalled lane.

Turn right here, following the lane past curious black and white farm buildings at Pen-Twy, then continue uphill passing young conifer plantations. Before reaching dilapidated old sheds and a dis-used windpump hidden by trees on the right, turn right through a metal gate. A pleasant track bears left through the trees of Common Wood leading to a gate and a quiet lane separating these woods and Kiln Ground Wood.

A right turn leads to an appealing house named 'The Wood' with its unspoilt barn, stable and coach house. Continue along the lane with its interesting hedgerow of sloes, hips and haws remaining amongst a few surviving autumnal oak and bramble leaves. Before a stone house turn left along an enclosed track, liable to be churned up in winter by horses' hooves. This track descends to cross a brook by a brisk but deepish ford, then climbs up and around to meet another metalled lane, which is followed to the left passing Woodbine Farm.

Now follow the remote lane on the left to Brilley Green. This small hamlet consists of a few isolated cottages and a disused Methodist Chapel founded in 1828 where a tiny graveyard is filled with 19th century tombs. Beyond the adjoining white cottage bear right up the bank, over a stile and along a right of way following the right hand hedge. Where the hedge ends bear left across the field to a stile. Keep ahead going diagonally across the next field, keeping right of the farm and barns at Pentre Farm. Cross the field gate, where the official way continues ahead to meet the farm lane, but we were requested to turn left and join the lane beside the farm.

This beautifully windproofed lane protected by high holly hedges is followed to the right, and soon leads to a telephone box by the roadside, where a left turn leads back to the start at Brilley church.

Snodhill Castle.

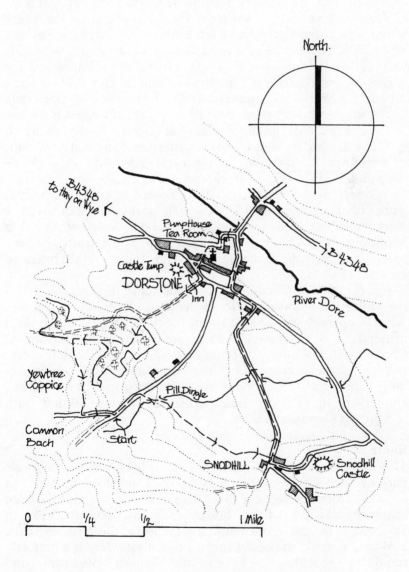

The attractive village of Dorstone nestles snugly near the banks of the river Dore at the northern end of the Golden Valley in west Herefordshire. The river gave its name to the valley, when the Normans translated the Welsh 'dwr' meaning water to 'd'or' the French for gold. Dorstone is six miles from the Welsh market town of Hay-on-Wye, and is sheltered by the foothills of the Black Mountains whose high ridges form the boundary between England and Wales. The eastern hills of Merbach and Dorstone rise steeply to 1000 feet offering extensive views of the Wye Valley and the Welsh borders. Nearby the inquisitive rambler may find Arthur's Stones, a prehistoric chambered tomb, the remains of which date back to the Neolithic period. It is under the care of English Heritage.

The centre of this charming village has grown between the church of St. Faith's and the remains of the castle motte and bailey. Groups of buildings including an inn, general store and Post Office surround a trim village green, where a plaque confirms that Dorstone won the Best Kept Village Award in 1974. An ancient stone column, surmounted by a sundial, marks the site of a former market shed which had disappeared by 1800. Near here stands a Methodist Chapel built of red brick in 1864 and a disused railway track once belonging to the Golden Valley Railway which operated between 1881 and 1957.

The beautiful undulating countryside south of Dorstone offers the walker an unlimited choice of delightful footpaths to explore, but a total lack of signs and a changing landscape make them difficult to find. Our enjoyable four mile ramble starting at Common Bach follows a bridleway leading to Snodhill where picturesque castle ruins still cling to a prominent hill. From here quiet lanes lead to Dorstone where refreshments may be obtained. Unmarked paths then lead across Greathouse Wood with spectacular views on all sides.

Route
This ramble starts at Common Bach where limited vergeside parking is available at GR 308406. Walk north along the lane towards Dorstone, within 300 yards turn right and follow an unsigned, clearly defined bridleway across several fields to Snodhill. Cross the wooden hurdle at the top of the bank where the sunken way leads to the delightful Pill Dingle. Here is a perfectly tranquil scene with spring bright water chattering over stones and gravel as it disappears under an ancient stone bridge.

The bridleway crosses this bridge and proceeds across a field to a gate beyond a muddy rock strewn corner. From the gate an enclosed track leads into level meadows divided by hurdles and gates. Keep left of the approaching farm where the track joins the road at Snodhill, a small hamlet in the parish of Peterchurch. In order to visit the picturesque ruins of Snodhill castle, turn right then immediately left opposite Pool Farm along the Peterchurch road. Pass the attractive 17th century stone built Court Farm, whose ancient stone brackets by the entrance may well have come from the castle.

The crumbling edifice is soon reached, its 12th century ruins standing in a lofty position above the Golden Valley. This Norman fortification belonged at one time to King Stephen but by the 1300s it came into the hands of the Chandos family. Having viewed the ruins retrace your way back to Pool Farm, then turn right and follow the pretty lane into Dorstone village.

Some marvellous views can be appreciated of low lying fields full of plover, chattering magpies and rooks playing in tall trees, all framed below the steep hills of Dorstone and Merbach. Where the road veers right take the footpath through the village cricket field to a wicket gate and across a garden to join the road. This right of way is unsigned at present so we decided to stick to the road which turns left at the junction and enters Dorstone.

From Dorstone Court follow the Peterchurch/Hereford road where the Jubilee Bridge leads across a tributary of the river Dore. Turn left at the main road where the attractive Pump House will be seen ahead.

Refreshment

The Pump House Tea and Craft Shop is arguably the best tea room in the Welsh Borders. It is run by Mrs. Goodman and her artist daughter, and it is very traditional. The 'house' is in fact a 17th century cottage with oak beams, whitewashed walls and a small lawn with a flower garden where on sunny days tired walkers and other visitors can sit at ease with their mouth watering cream scones, home made jam and pots of Earl Grey tea.

The Pump House is much appreciated by its diverse customers, 'we drove 30 miles to return to this haven' was spotted in the visitors book when we called. The fare is prepared in the neat Rayburn warmed kitchen. There is no set tea but ramblers are invited to eat as much as they like from the menu containing such delights as wholemeal honey scones, hot Welsh cakes, sliced loaf cake and chocolate crunchy biscuits. The coffee is freshly ground and there is a selection of teas and natural fruit juices.

Children's portions are available and nice touches include the advice not to feed Patsy, the friendly family pet rescued from the Battersea Dog's Home, the offer of low cholesterol butter and the toilets which have been converted to accommodate the handicapped and elderly. Customers are clearly in caring hands at the Pump House which is open most of the year from 10.00 to 12.30 and 2.30 to 5.30 but closed all day Wednesday. Books, cards and prints, many from the scraper-board of Mrs. Goodman's daughter, are on sale with various examples of craftsmen's skills. A good alternative refreshment place is at *The Pandy Inn* overlooking the village green offering a range of interesting snacks, main meals and real ale.

Return

The return route continues pleasantly by turning left from the Pump House. Carefully negotiate the bends of the main road till reaching the parish church of St. Faith. Its solid square tower, crowded graveyard and old yew trees suggest an ancient site, and although the church was founded in 1256 it was entirely rebuilt in 1889. Walk through the graveyard to a swing gate and follow a quiet lane across a brook, where stone steps lead to the water's edge. In the heart of Dorstone one can fully appreciate the timelessness of narrow lanes and old dwellings huddled prettily around the village green which suns itself beneath the tree-topped hills accompanied by the cheerful chirping of birds.

The 17th century timber framed Pandy Inn has a name that indicates its association with a local fulling mill. Here turn left along the road and before reaching a house called Hafod follow the lane on the right signed 'No Through Road'. The wooded mound of Dorstone's castle can still be seen, alas only scanty remains are all that is left of this motte and bailey castle which also belonged to the Chandos family. Ahead loom the hills of Mill Wood and Greathouse Wood. While the lane veers right towards the site of Dorstone Mill, our way continues ahead.

The path crossing Greathouse and Mill Woods is not clearly defined, and from the siting of the stiles and gates it does not strictly follow the line on the definitive map. Cross the gate ahead and where the field broadens bear diagonally left, climbing very steeply through cleared woodland where ash, beech and oak trees grow between huge piles of rotting roots. The hill top offers breathtaking and panoramic views of Dorstone surrounded by fertile fields lying below wooded hills. Bear left to a gate leading into the adjoining field. Turn sharp right alongside the fence to the corner where a new stile will be found on your left. From here a clear path leads through mixed woodland to a rusty gate.

At this point leave the woods and bear slightly left diagonally across undulating pastures and through the remains of a hedgerow keeping left of the inappropriately named Yewtree Coppice. Here clear views of Snodhill castle surrounded by the beautiful Golden Valley may be enjoyed. Proceed straight ahead to the corner where a stile stands to the right of a small pond. Still keeping ahead walk through a wooded grove churned up by horses hooves and squeeze through a gap in the hedge. Cross the field walking towards and to the right of a stone cottage, where a wooden stile leads onto a bank with an unusual old stone stile taking one onto the lane. Turn left and return to the car.

7 BREINTON SPRING

OS Sheet 149

8 miles

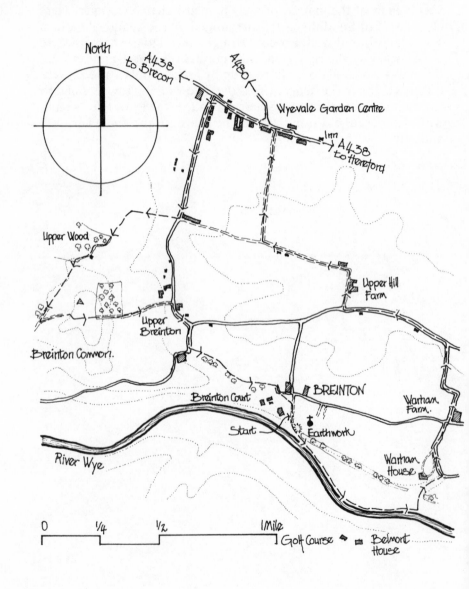

Only three miles west of the cathedral city of Hereford stands a low oval mound overlooking the river Wye at Breinton. Recent excavations here have established that it was a moated site occupied during the 1100s but abandoned the following century. Earlier research suggested a much earlier earthwork of the iron age period built to defend the sunken trackway leading to an ancient ford. This river crossing was still in use in the 1800s when a local farmer conveyed his belongings and livestock across the Wye to Lower Breinton.

A most interesting and attractive feature here is the crystal clear spring water which tumbles from the rocky base of the sandstone mound. This supply of pure and natural water never fails even during the driest of summers, providing one with a free and refreshing drink. This incidentally gives the site its name, Breinton Spring, now in the care of the National Trust who have constructed a car park. Across the orchard one can see the parish church of Breinton with its unusual slate spire. Dedicated to St. Michael it dates back to the 12th century, but was practically rebuilt by F.R. Kempson in the late 1860s.

This is essentially an undemanding walk suitable for the whole family, encompassing river bank, pasture land, orchards and country lanes. We found the route unexpectedly well signed by the parish council and the Country Landowners Association whose 'Welcome Careful Walkers' waymarks made the walk easy to follow. The views are sweeping rather than dramatic with lovely long stretches of the river Wye and large fields dotted here and there with elderly oaks. The naturalist is well catered for with sightings of wild geese, swans and herons plus the usual delightful array of interesting British birds more often seen in the Herefordshire countryside.

From Breinton Spring a pleasant stretch of the Wye is followed before a gentle ascent to Warham, where quiet winding lanes and a succession of defined bridleways lead to the refreshment break at Wyevale Garden Centre. The return footpaths climb to Breinton Common and Upper Breinton where more varied and extensive scenes are visible.

Route

This walk begins at the National Trust car park (GR 472395) adjacent to the church at Breinton. A selection of paths lead from the rustic gate around, across or below the sparsely wooded earthwork which can be investigated before sampling the gushing spring water near the riverside. The right of way goes left along the banks of the Wye following a well used path through fields and over

47

a variety of stiles. The scenery here is typical of the middle Wye Valley, steep wooded slopes rising above riverside meadows providing ideal haunts for heron and wild geese. On the opposite bank the tall gabled Victorian mansion of Belmont together with its attractive parkland has in recent years been transformed into a beautifully landscaped eighteen hole golf course and club house.

After passing Belmont House turn left away from the river, immediately before the footbridge indicated by a waymark. Keep to the right hand hedge between a break in the trees to pass the red bricked Warham House. Bear right to another stile leading onto a lane which is followed to the left. Old hedgerows covered with snow were difficult to identify but hazel, bramble and elder were noticed. At a minor crossroads keep straight ahead with the rambling barns and sheds of Warham Farm on the right. For about half a mile this quiet lane winds around sharp bends, and it is hard to imagine that one is but two miles from the bustling city of Hereford. In the distance the Victorian tower of the Broomy Hill Waterworks still stands above the Pumping Station built in 1856 to supply Hereford with drinking water. This now houses a fascinating Waterworks Museum.

At the next junction follow a lane to the left between large fields sheltered by coppices, solitary oaks and orchards. Many buildings in the area are red brick including this isolated dwelling called Halfway House. A restored cider mill and press stand prominently outside the entrance to Little Breinton, within yards of this follow the signed bridleway on the right leading past Upper Hill Farm. Beyond the farm buildings, Country Landowners Association waymarks are followed to the left between a wayside pool and a derelict cottage.

This is a well defined bridleway known as Green Lane which passes further dwellings and a radio mast before it narrows, nearly disappearing beneath high hedges beside the well spaced trees in Green Lane Wood. At a crossways turn sharp right along a wide and straight bridlepath leading to Kings Acre. Views of Credenhill can now be seen, standing at nearly 700 feet where iron age man built their hill fort. At Kings Acre cross the Hereford to Brecon road to the Wyevale Garden Centre.

Refreshment
The Wyevale Garden Centre is a splendid tea stop, airy and light with bamboo and cane decor set in a corner of the Nursery amid bulbs, books and gardening utensils. The food here is inexpensive,

quick and pleasantly served. A varied menu includes fishy dishes like scampi, cod and plaice all served with chips, peas and tomato. Soup of the day with a sandwich is usually enough for even the most ravenous walker, but there is also a dish of the day featuring, the day we inspected, steak and kidney pie.

Coffee is fluffy freshly made Expresso, tea includes Earl Grey and there is a selection of soft drinks and a simple wine list. Vegetarians are not forgotten, there are lots of non meat dishes including salads and quiches. The sweet cabinet is crammed with such fattening, mouth watering favourites as apple pies and meringues all smothered in fresh cream. The service is swift and pleasant and everything is spotlessly clean, even odd stray crumbs are expertly 'hoovered' by the cheeky sparrows which have learnt to gain entrance to such a tempting haven.

A number of retired people use this particular tea shop on a regular basis, and what better way to while away a long day than by tucking into a nice lunch or tea then exploring the stock of bulbs, seeds, plants, tools and books. The Wyevale opens all the year around from nine to half past four except Christmas and Boxing Day. There is plenty of car parking space and good toilet facilities. The only alternative is an inn found 500 yards down the road towards Hereford. *The Bay Horse* is a comfortable little pub full of bric a brac and brasses. The menu is quite adequate with substantial bar snacks and Whitbread's range of beers.

Return
Leaving this excellent tea stop walk along the main road towards Brecon for nearly 500 yards to the turn on the left signed Breinton. A group of new houses, bungalows and another Garden Centre line the left hand side of this tarmaced lane. Opposite some cottages take the next clearly signed footpath identified by its new sign and stile. This path keeps to the right hand hedge through two fields, then naturally bears left following the waymarks. A short climb up a field to a point alongside Upper Wood offers more commanding views. A stile in the right hand corner leads onto an old overgrown track which is followed over fallen trees for a short stretch to a gate. Now in the adjoining parish of Stretton Sugwas the Country Landowners Association waymarks are sadly absent, however the official right of way follows the left hand hedge skirting a neglected pool, then follows a line to the right of a disused track leading to derelict ivy clad ruins known as Park Croft.

The footpath continues across stiles, but before reaching wooded slopes near Breinton Common, one ought to pause for a moment to admire the best view point on this ramble. Hills of Garnons, Wormsley and Credenhill are visible above the wandering Wye, whose opposite bank is dominated by a large red bricked house at Lower Eaton. The footpath now briefly enters mixed woodland to a stile bearing the now familiar waymarks. Turn sharp left along an enclosed lane through a gate onto a well marked birdleway.

Keep close to the right hand hedge till the end of the meadow, then carefully proceed left across the next field to join an enclosed track leading to farms and barns at Upper Breinton. On the day we were walking huge piles of snow had drifted against the hedges, and we had fun identifying numerous claw and paw marks. At the road turn right past a group of interesting dwellings, ignore a left turn before joining a waymarked footpath on the left. Cross the brook, climb the bank and step over a new stile. Keep to the right hand hedge through the field to another stile and continue to a swing gate in the corner of the next field after passing tall pines surrounding Breinton Court. Bear right here beside a cottage, cross a private lane, go through an iron gate and diagonally across an orchard to return to the car park opposite Breinton House.

8 SKENFRITH CASTLE

3½ miles

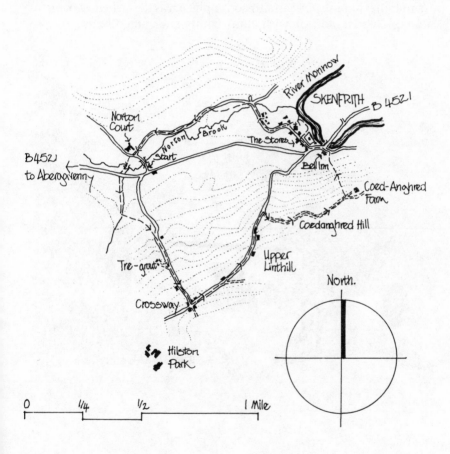

Skenfrith lies within a mile of the Welsh Borders in the county of Gwent. It sits pleasantly on the banks of the river Monnow, and the hills of Garway, Graig Syfyrddin and Coedanghred make a dramatic backcloth to this idyllic village. Visitors and locals alike can explore the ruined castle, visit the 13th century church, inspect the water mill, view the arts and crafts and enjoy the hospitality of the tea room and pub. These tidy and well kept buildings stand outside the rough stone walls of the Norman castle, and it is difficult to imagine that in 1904 this attractive place was described as being in a dilapidated condition with many empty and ruined houses.

St Bridget's Church, Skenfrith.

The castle was constructed during the 11th century to defend a main route from England into Wales. From the reign of Henry II it became known as one of 'The Three Castles' together with

52

nearby Grosmont and White castles, which were in common ownership throughout the medieval period. The church standing alongside was built in 1207 and dedicated to the celtic St. Bridget.

This is a delightfully undulating stroll of less than four miles, taking the rambler along narrow lanes, through old pastures and up bracken clad hills. Everywhere there are stunning views including an almost aerial scene of the red sandstone village of Skenfrith bordered by the swift flowing Monnow. On a sunny day when the views are crystal clear this is a most enjoyable area for walking. The paths are generally in good condition with only one or two awkward places. It is also steeped in history, so do allow extra time to investigate some fascinating sites along the way.

Route
Cars can be parked along the verges near Norton Court at the crossroads (GR 446200). Opposite the stone buildings of the Court cross a gate, and walk through a meadow to a wooden footbridge, attractively built on large stone boulders. Having crossed the winding Norton Brook continue ahead to another gate leading onto the Abergavenny road. Cross the road and gate where the undefined footpath keeps to the left hand side of the field alongside the brook. Continue until reaching a gate and footbridge on the left. From here the line of the path crosses the fields to the left of the tall building of Tre-gout seen on the skyline. Ascend the slope and walk towards a cottage called The Garth, which now comes into view. At the time of writing you have to squeeze through the thick hedge to reach the road at The Garth, but a stile will soon be erected by the local authority.

Turn right along the road up the steep pitch, passing a cottage of that name, to Crossway, a junction of roads surrounded by a group of houses and cottages including a Police Station. Follow the metal lane on the left where several isolated dwellings are seen. Behind the trees on the right stands Hilston Park, which was for many years the principal mansion and estate in the parish of St. Maughan's. The lane descends past Upper Linthill becoming shady with tall hedgerows of hazel, ash, hawthorn and blackthorn all clad with ivy. Away from the trees one can admire the pleasant sight of Garway Hill easily identified by its radio mast, and the wooded hills of the Graig.

The next track on the right is followed which leads to an interesting and mysterious place, the Roman Catholic Burial Ground at Coedanghred. Beyond the steps and iron railings on the right, beneath an eerie canopy of yews, lean gravestones of the last and present centuries. In spite of its atmosphere we were surprised to learn that the burial ground and church were only founded in 1844. The church was demolished in 1911, after only 55 years of worship, when many local Catholic families left the district.

At the end of the track take the left hand gate to follow an irregular path over Coedanghred Hill, meaning 'wood of unbelief'. The rough hillside consists of bracken, thistles, reeds and marshland where the right of way keeps to the contours towards Coed-Anghred Farm. An iron hurdle is crossed, and from here there is a superb view of Skenfrith with its church and castle surrounded by a cluster of attractive dwellings and the river Monnow. Walk across a cultivated field and before reaching the hilltop farm turn sharp left at an oak tree. Ahead you will eventually find a makeshift stile in the hedge, where the footpath goes down hill through fields keeping to the left hand hedges.

While descending there is a fine view of the triple arched bridge spanning the Monnow, this was built in 1824 replacing an earlier structure. Cross a stile beside the Bell Inn, walk through a small area of bracken and climb a high gate leading onto the road beside the pub. At this quiet corner of Skenfrith one can watch the swirling Monnow behind lush banks of Himalayan Balsam, Horseradish and a variety of reeds. Groups of sunbathing mallards can be seen nearly indistinguishable from the colour of the brown rocks that they rest on. Nearby is the site of St. Fraed's Well, which we failed to locate, although it is clearly marked on the map.

Turn left along the road passing the unusual combination of war memorial and drinking fountain, behind stands Skenfrith Mill. It is now driven by electricity although the sack hoist is worked by an undershot water wheel powered by the Monnow. Since the 13th century there has been a water mill at Skenfrith. Bear right through the village where the Stores and Tea Room will be found opposite the castle walls.

Refreshments

The Stores is a welcome watering hole, stocking everything from pet foods to papers, free range eggs to instant soup. The shop is thriving and its owners are kept on their toes by the demands of visitors who throng to the castle during the summer. Tucked away beside the shop is a small tea room which seats about twenty on a busy day. Rush matted and comfortable with items of local craftmanship, ranging from Welsh hand-knitted cardies to quite respectable paintings displayed around the walls. It is a cosy place to enjoy a cup of tea and a warm Welsh cake. Cream teas and toast are also available and there are soft drinks and ice creams for the children. Ramblers are made to feel at home, and several local guides may be purchased in the shop. After this leisurely ramble a cup of strong tea, while watching customers purchasing their Welsh dolls or little moulded owls, is a pleasant way to spend half an hour. The tea room is closed September to Easter.

The Bell Inn is placed strategically at the foot of the hill near Skenfrith bridge. It is a homely pub with a range of meals and plenty of choice among the beverages. There is a lawn where kids may swing while their parents or guardians rest clutching something sustaining. The inn, of course, is open all the year round.

Return

Now refreshed it is time to explore the ruins of the Norman castle with its remaining gatehouse, corner towers, prominent round tower and outline of its western range of chambers. Since the 1500s the building has lain derelict, but since the National Trust obtained the property in 1936 the site has been cleared and much conservation work has been undertaken. Further history and description of this ancient monument can be read in the Official Guide available at the Stores.

Leaving the castle turn right through the gate into the riverside meadow and make for the banks of the Monnow, where the noisy weir can be seen and heard. This, of course, is necessary to steer the water along the willow lined leat to power the mill. Follow the bank to the left for a few yards, then left again towards the church into an outer graveyard where sheep graze around the crumbling tombs. Cross a stile into the churchyard and enter this lively old church by a massive oak studded door. Tower, nave, chancel and altar stone date back to the 13th century with many later additions. It is full of interesting features, notably, John Morgan's Tomb, the Cope embroidered in the 15th century, the Morgan Pew of the Jacobean period, and the ancient stone font. More information may be gleaned from the excellent guide on sale by the entrance.

A seat sheltered by a large yew growing into the walls of the churchyard is seen when leaving. Turn right along the metal lane passing the old National School built in 1843 and the handsome old Vicarage. There are fine views here of the hills between Skenfrith and Grosmont before reaching Malt House Farm and the prettily situated Drybridge House. This narrow lane with its hedgerows of plum, blackberry, hazel and lilac was the main road to Abergavenny before the construction of the present highway in the 1820s. The lane crosses the Norton Brook, and a footpath is followed through a gate on the left, across the field with the hay barn on the right. Enter the next field by a gate with unusual rustic posts, then turn sharp right to cross a hurdle in the hedge leading back onto the lane.

Turn left along the lane beside the chattering Norton Brook which is bordered by pleasant pastures below the hill of Coedanghred. Enjoy the remainder of this tranquil scene because Norton Court and the end of the walk is soon reached.

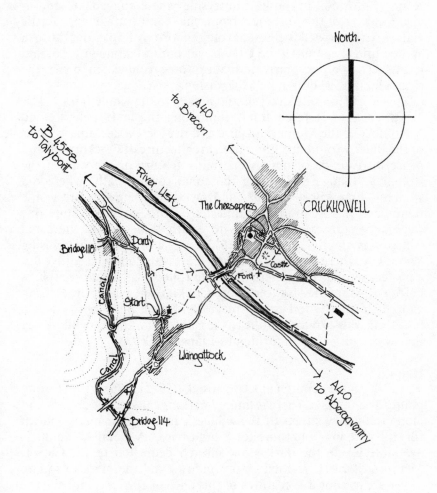

North.

to Brecon A40

B 4558 to Talybont

River Usk

The Cheesepress

CRICKHOWELL

Bridge 116

Dardy

Canal

Start

Ford

Castle

Llangattock

Canal

Bridge 114

to Abergavenny A40

0   ¼   ½   1 Mile

The dignified and well preserved small country town of Crickhowell lies within the Brecon Beacons National Park in the Welsh county of Powys. Beneath the flat topped Table Mountain (1481 feet) the town overlooks the stony river Usk flowing purposefully past on its journey to Abergavenny. This is typical border scenery, glorious unspoilt countryside where rugged mountains disappear into the distance from the comfortable and fertile valleys. Crickhowell is entered from the west by a splendid thirteen arched bridge spanning the Usk. It was built of stone in 1706, and its attractive parapets provide an ideal stage from which to view the riverside, the fishermen and the gushing weir.

This level five mile stroll should appeal to the whole family. It is as varied as it is fascinating, combining the leafy delights and tranquility of the Monmouthshire and Brecon Canal, superb views of the Black Mountains, the varied architecture of Crickhowell and peaceful riverside scenes. A charming feature of the walk is the stretch at Llangattock along the canal towing path, where old wharves, lime kilns, cottages and picturesque bridges are gentle reminders of past industrial times. Iron ore, coal and limestone were once conveyed by barges to South Wales along the canal which was finally opened in 1812. It is now called a Cruising Waterway where boating, canoeing and fishing may be enjoyed in a perfect setting. From here the route follows lanes and footpaths before crossing the Usk to explore Crickhowell with its interesting church, host of good eating places and pleasant shops. After a break the walker may visit the castle ruins and wander awhile along the riverbank before returning to Llangattock.

Route

The 12th century church at Llangattock (GR 211179) is the starting point for our walk. There is limited parking outside the church and along the pretty streets of the village, which was formerly known for its weaving and limestone industries. A detailed guide is available inside the dark stone church dedicated to St. Catwg. Memorial tablets, stained glass windows and the massive square tower are memorable features of this ancient edifice. Opposite the lych gate there is a working water fountain erected by a local benefactor in 1881. From here bear left along the cobbled pavement, passing rows of attractive cottages and cross the narrow Omneu Brook. At a T junction turn right along the road to the Bethesda Independent Chapel founded in 1835.

Keep left at the chapel where the road shortly reaches the

Monmouthshire and Brecon Canal. To join the tow path bear left before bridge (numbered 114) and climb over a tricky stile composed of steep stone steps. For those not so sprightly turn right at the chapel where the tarmac lane meets the tow path at a more convenient place. This is a very pleasant mile stroll along the banks of the canal, first passing the lime kilns and colourful boats moored at Llangattock Wharf, where more conservatively attired ducks enjoy the stillness and privacy of the water. On the right under some tall trees stands a Great Western Railway boundary marker, placed here by the railway company who owned the canal before its decline.

The Monmouthshire and Brecon Canal.

On approaching the next bridge there are fine views of Crickhowell with its prominent church compactly sited below the Black Mountain range, including Table Mountain called Crug Hywwel from which the town's name is derived. Before the attractive stone bridge there is an old fashioned stile leading to a suitably placed seat overlooking the town. Walk below the arch of this bridge and under the following footbridge, then continue along the path where steep banks are lined with oaks, alders, chestnuts and sycamores. All clad with thick ivy they make an ideal cover for the jackdaws, magpies, robins and blue tits who also enjoy the fresh water trickling happily from the hidden feeder spring. Along this stretch we were lucky to watch a gaily painted narrow boat glide by from Gilwern.

At the next hump-backed canal bridge (numbered 118), one almost regretfully leaves the towing path by crossing the stone stile and turning sharp right down a metalled lane to meet the road at Dardy. Bear right along this road, around the bend to a footpath sign on the left indicating the way past a row of renovated cottages at Cwrt-isaf. Ahead, through an iron swing gate, the path crosses a field to join the main road beside the babbling and stone-cluttered Omneu Brook. In a neighbouring field horses and donkeys graze, timelessly providing a pleasant scene. Turn right along the main Abergavenny road, but before crossing the river Usk stop awhile to enjoy the splendid stone bridge spanning the river over thirteen arches, then turn left into Crickhowell.

Ahead, stands the Bridge End Inn with one half looking like a former toll house. Walk along New Road, constructed in 1830, which made an easier route through the town when it was on the coaching road between London and West Wales. Within a short distance bear right up steep stone steps to the loftily positioned church of St. Edmunds. The 700 year old building has many attractions including a memorial to the 17th century Jones family who lost twelve of their thirteen children in infancy, a stone tablet listing the Degrees of Marriage and 'Free' signs on the rear pews. Leave the churchyard by the archway dated 1843 and turn right along Church Street and Silver Lane passing the modern library before reaching the Square, where refreshments may be enjoyed at the Cheesepress.

Refreshments
The Cheesepress is a perfect halt for the weary walker. With its neat check clothed pine tables, it offers a clean and comfortable place for our well deserved break. The menu is fairly comprehensive listing

sandwiches, salads and quiches with the accent leaning towards the wholesomely homemade. A wide variety of sweetmeats include heavy slabs of boiled fruit cake and sweet biscuits. Homespun and independent the Cheesepress also offers Lasagne Verdi, potato cakes and herb tea, without which no Guardian reader would feel replete. However, Telegraphs were also seen enjoying the home-made fare and there is a smoking section for those nowadays treated as pariahs in most places. The café is only part of Cheesepress's business, tucked away as it is at the rear of a well stocked shop whose book titles suggest a non-nuclear, vegetarian bias, and an all round sensible attitude to life in general. There are lots of local guides too, and a nice line in potted preserves, herbs and honey. Wine is sold but this was not an obsession judging by the selection available. Hours of opening are nine to five except Sundays which is noon to five.

There is certainly no shortage of eating places in this pleasant little town. Nearby famished ramblers may prefer to try the following.

The Bear Hotel an ancient coach house.

The Corn Exchange a pub opposite the Cheesepress.

Dragon Hotel a cheerfully pink building further down on the left.

Return

From the Cheesepress walk to the centre of the Square identified by its Victorian water fountain commemorating Henry John Lucas 1804 – 1873, a well loved local doctor. Continue along Standard Street leaving the town centre behind, turn left following Greenhill Way to its junction with the main road, and proceed right again along the main road before crossing over to a clearly defined footpath leading to the castle ruins. Sited between the Cricket Club pitch and children's playground, the castle bears a plaque reminding us that this pleasant public park and ancient ruins were given by Gwilym C. James Esq. late of Llanwysg, in memory of his son who died in the First World War. These ruins are called Alisby's Castle after an early governor of this Norman castle built in 1272.

Walk towards the Presbyterian Chapel rebuilt in its present attractive style in 1829, turn left along Castle Street and rejoin the main road, which is followed to the right for about 200 yards. Before the small industrial estate cross a stile on the right and walk diagonally left across the field to a further stile behind the new factory. From here the footpath continues in a straight line to the banks of the river Usk.

The beautiful Usk, noted for its salmon and trout fishing, rises on the northern slopes of the Black Mountains and flows through important border towns of Brecon and Abergavenny before pouring into the mouth of the Severn at Newport. At the riverside turn right and follow its willow lined banks where a well worn path crosses a series of stiles on the way to Crickhowell Bridge. The more adventurous (or plain foolhardy) may ford the river by a public bridleway which leads from a point opposite the 19th century Baptist Chapel. Otherwise turn left over the bridge, cross the main road and follow the signed footpath directly opposite. A tarmac path leads through fields, eventually crossing a miniature stone bridge over the trout filled Omneu Brook before returning to the church of St. Catwg's at Llangattock.

10 GREAT DOWARD

4½ miles

OS Sheet 162

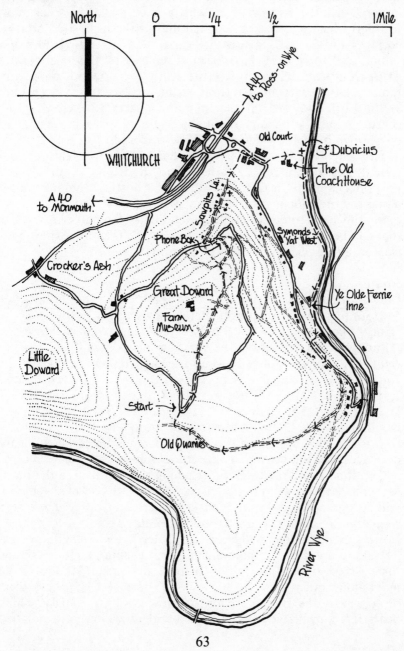

North

0   ¼   ½   1 Mile

A 40 to Ross-on-Wye

Old Court

St Dubricius

WHITCHURCH

The Old Coach House

A 40 to Monmouth.

Sawpits La.

Phone Box

Symonds Yat West

Crocker's Ash

Great Doward

Ye Olde Ferrie Inne

Farm Museum

Little Doward

Start

Old Quarries

River Wye

The Great and Little Doward are wooded hills reaching to over 600 feet, and lie to the south of Herefordshire with outstanding views over the neighbouring counties of Gwent and Gloucestershire. The larger Doward is criss-crossed with a maze of lanes, tracks and footpaths leading between isolated and attractively sited houses, cottages and farms. The area has varied and interesting flora and fauna, and forty acres have been purchased by the local Nature Trust as a protected reserve. Historically the Dowards date from remains left by early man at King Arthur's Cave, and iron age man at the Little Doward. Stone, lime and quarry workers over the centuries have left many fascinating underground passages and overgrown quarries which can still be explored.

This energetic ramble passes several interesting features and tourist sites. It is extremely varied, changing from the solitude and unspoilt beauty of the Great Doward to the bustling commercialism along the riverside at Symonds Yat West. Across the Doward the directions need to be closely followed due to the numerous routes that can be taken, but from the banks of the river Wye the way is clearer, although considerably steeper on the return.

Route
Park in the Forestry Commission car park called the Biblins (GR 546156) then walk back to the metal lane which is followed to the right. Follow this for a few hundred yards to a track ahead signed 'Heritage Museum', leave the winding lane which bears sharply right. On your left you will notice the entrance to Leeping Stocks Nature Reserve which was purchased by the Herefordshire and Radnorshire Nature Trust in 1975 with help from the World Wildlife Fund. The reserve consists mainly of scrub and deciduous woodland where 130 plant species have been recorded. Toadstools flourish in the autumn and foxes and badgers breed here. Please note access to the reserve is only for members.

Continue along the track till reaching the entrance to the Farm Museum, where a collection of tractors, horsedrawn vehicles, vintage engines and domestic machines are on display. Here bear right, ignore all turns and enjoy the scenery and the variety of flowers in the summer hedgerows. At a derelict white building turn left along a concreted lane, and before reaching a stone cottage turn sharp right and follow a pleasant green lane offering marvellous open views of the Welsh Borders. The view soon disappears as the route descends to follow a holly lined path, which bears left and arrives at the road beside a white cottage called

64

Martyns Heron. Standing opposite is the only telephone box on the Doward.

Follow the road to the left for about 200 yards where an even narrower road is met on the right, justifying its 'Unauthorised for Motors' sign. Known as Sawpits Lane, also the name of the cottage on the left. Again one can briefly enjoy uninterrupted views towards Wales before descending between high banks lined with blackberries, gooseberries, hazel, ferns, Honesty and Rose of Sharon. Carry on until reaching the chapel on the hill.

The way continues up some inviting stone steps, through a wrought iron gate into the graveyard of the United Reform Church, which was founded in 1816 as a Congregational Chapel. Before leaving do not miss the brief undated inscription on a white tombstone 'James and Annie Reece, at Peace'. Further steps lead out of the graveyard where a nicely placed seat allows another opportunity to enjoy the scenery.

Turn left through an iron swing gate, keep to the right-hand hedge through a large sloping meadow towards the brash activities of Symonds Yat West, a popular tourist resort in the parish of Whitchurch. The Wye Valley Visitor Centre has the Jubilee Maze, World of Butterflies and a Souvenir Shop, and the Leisure Park offers boat trips, amusements and a Bird Park. On reaching the road by a further iron swing gate, turn right between the Visitor Centre and Old Court, a large 16th and 17th century house now used as a hotel. Leave this busy area behind by taking a left hand lane to St. Dubricius church. It also leads to the refreshment stop.

Refreshments
The Old Coach House is conveniently situated about half way round the walk, and just before the steepest part. It is a much modernised, and at the time of writing unfinished, old building with ample room on the patio if weather permits. Under large umbrellas, useful also in the rain, one can enjoy a pot of strong tea or a cup of coffee with a wedge of homemade gateau, which comes in a variety of flavours, Banana, Coffee, and would you believe — Passion Fruit. If absolutely starving there is a fairly comprehensive snack menu, listing such delights as Curry, Home Baked Ham and various Salads. Soft drinks and ice creams for the kids are also available.

It is a quiet spot in spite of the adjacent camp site, and while awaiting service there are a few weird looking sculptures lying about, upon which an artistic eye may roam. It is worth mentioning here that the Coach House closes from September to Easter, and as any rambler worth his or her salt is an all-the-year-rounder, then it might be wise to list a few alternatives.

The Old Court Hotel advertises Cream Teas plus of course a range of meals and stronger cordials for those so interested.

Ye Olde Ferrie Inne, a riverside pub, found a little further on in the walk. It provides food and drink associated with this type of establishment.

Return

From the tea room continue towards the church, founded in Saxon times and dedicated to St. Dubricius a Welsh Bishop and teacher in the 6th century. There are some 13th and 14th century remains in the church which was partially restored in 1860. Outside stands the ancient preaching cross, a centuries old Tulip tree and an interesting and unusually spacious vault in memory of the Gwillim family, who lived at Old Court in the 17th and 18th centuries. Cross the graveyard to the banks of the river Wye, where a landing stage is a reminder of those who came to church by boat.

At the Wye turn right along the riverside path where campers, canoeists and boat trippers intermingle with the willows, water fowl and scenic beauty of the rocky and woody gorge ahead. At Ye Olde Ferrie Inne, reputed to be 500 years old, leave the river and walk up the quaint steps through an archway on the right of the inn.

Now at the upper level turn left along a track till reaching Cammdwr. Beyond this cottage a steep ascent begins. Climb the steps and slippery footpath on the right, leading up to the higher road, which is then followed to the left.

Before this road descends again to reach the Wye Rapids Hotel, keep ahead along a narrow but well defined path which eventually widens. Pass some half hidden lime kilns and another reserve purchased by the World Wildlife Fund for the Woodland Trust. This is an area of steep cliffs and old quarries covered with creepers, moss and ferns. At the wide waymarked forest track, take the right hand fork passing the Pancake Mines, an interesting area of caves and old mine workings, where a torch and great care should be taken if explored. Glimpses of the Wye at New Weir can be seen through the trees, where the iron ore was manufactured at a forge powered by the river water. It was used from the 17th century till just before 1820, when the extensive iron works became dilapidated and were abandoned.

Almost immediately after spotting a cave entrance, with a dark and dangerous drop, turn sharply right beside a spreading Beech

66

tree, leaving the waymarked trail to follow a stony track through mixed woodland. Take the first left and at a ruined building bear left along a main path, passing a deep mine shaft on your left, which is surrounded by a wire fence. Several isolated houses are soon reached, the path widens, and after one cottage called White Rocks, a gentle ascent leads to the forestry road, where the Biblins car park will be found on the left.

11 CANNOP PONDS
6½ miles

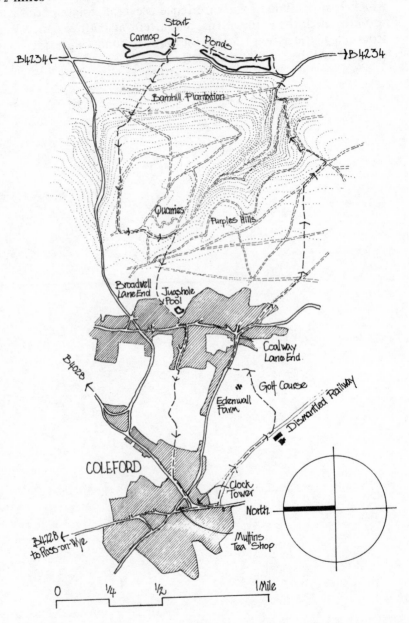

The Royal Forest of Dean is a beautiful and fascinating area lying between the rivers Wye and Severn in the county of Gloucestershire. In a long and interesting history it has provided man with much of his basic needs – iron ore, timber, charcoal, coal and animals for hunting. During the 19th century up to a million tons of coal a year was mined from the Forest pits. This huge amount was transported by a network of tramroads and railways whose disused tracks can be investigated today. A gradual change took place this century transforming this once industrial site into a scenic forest managed by the Forestry Commission since 1923.

The Cannop Ponds are a pair of placid pools surrounded by delightful woodland. They were man made in the early 1800s to provide water power for iron works at Parkend. At this time a chemical works at the Cannop crossroads was producing wood tar, pitch, acetate and sulphuric acid till its closure in 1902. A few years later the Cannop Colliery opened and remained in operation until 1960. The ponds are now an attractive feature used for recreational purposes. The Forestry Commission have provided parking, a picnic site, an information board and waymarked forest trails. Fishermen enjoy the rich selection of tench, bream, perch, chub and roach while walkers and horse riders appreciate the wonderful choice of paths and tracks leading into the cool deep forest.

From Cannop Ponds our six to seven mile ramble follows a waymarked route steeply climbing the tree clad slopes of Barnhill Plantation. At Bixslade Quarry a mixture of fairly level tracks, lanes, roads and footpaths lead to Broadwell and on to Coleford, the main tourist town in the Forest of Dean. Here our refreshment stop is found, after which we press on to Coalway before returning through a delightful part of the forest.

Route
The Forestry Commission carpark at Cannop Ponds (GR 610107) is the beginning of this woodland walk. Leave the picnic area where rustic tables and benches are temptingly arranged beside the water's edge. Cross a bridge over a shallow brook connecting the two ponds, in summer it provides an ideal paddling pool for toddlers, and follow the raised path waymarked with yellow arrows. On the ponds, frozen when we visited, we caught only a glimpse of coot identified by its white front and moorhen with red markings, also numerous seagulls forced inland by the extremely cold weather sliding uncomfortably on the glassy surface.

At the road the waymarked path continues ahead, bearing left into a dark deep conifer planation lit only by flashes of sun slanting through the trees. Cross a main track where the path meanders over a series of ditches. This well used route is clearly defined and gently ascends into even deeper woods before another main track is crossed. Now the path widens as it steeply climbs to the top of Barnhill Plantation beside the overgrown cliffs of a disused quarry. The forest is more open here, oak, fir, cypresses, silver birch, beech, hazel and chestnut trees grow above a thick carpet of bracken. Soon a spruce plantation on the right cushions the path with decades of soft needles.

At the next forest track turn sharply right as indicated by a yellow arrow, but at the crossways leave the waymarked route by turning left along a wide stone paved track proving that it was once a tramroad leading from the large quarries at Bixslade, which are soon reached. Here three quarries have been worked for five hundred years producing Pennant Sandstone used to construct the Gloucester Shire Hall, the Severn Tunnel and the Severn Railway Tunnel in the 1800s. More recently this stone was used to build the Berkeley Power Station and the University Colleges of Wales and London. Keep in between these deep and dangerous excavations, and be careful if you peer over the treacherously steep sides. Shortly leave this intriguing melange of cranes, boulders and cliffs, by turning sharply right following a line of telegraph poles. A short sharp climb leads past a young plantation on the left before another main track is crossed. Keep ahead to pass a modern electricity generating station and the scattered houses and cottages at Broadwell.

On the outskirts of the village turn left along Bixhead Walk with stone cottages on the right, and rough land on the left where Jugshold Pool is reputed to be the site where foresters once obtained clay to make their jugs. On meeting the road continue left for about thirty yards then right along Queensway, a small housing estate. At the end of this road cross the stile and follow a well trodden footpath going straight across the fields towards Coleford. On this section there are commanding views of the Welsh hills at Monmouth and Trellech and an elevated view of Coleford town.

At a stile bear left and proceed downhill alongside rugby pitches to the outskirts of Coleford. On meeting the Gloucester Road turn left through the town with its varied shops, inns, banks, a Tourist Information Centre and a good book shop. The centre is prominently marked with an odd clock tower, all that remains of a church demolished in 1882. Turn right here along St. John Street to find our tea shop on the right.

Refreshment

The Muffins Tea Shop clearly thrives on local trade where plenty of couples tuck into the home produced fare. Muffins is a bright and pleasantly appointed place with white furniture, brown oilcloth and dried flowers in vases. The accent is on the freshly prepared which is admirable. The menu is not lengthy but more than adequate with a variety of tasty items listed. We tried the homemade Pizzas and they fitted the bill nicely. The basic Pizza with cheese may be supplemented by the 'extras' a scattering of mushrooms, ham and onions. Soup is freshly made, and there is a selection of sandwiches made with scrumptious granary bread and jacket potatoes with curry fillings.

If that is not enough ramblers who rush to Muffins before the eleven o'clock deadline may fill themselves with a good English breakfast at a derisory cost. Drinks include Cona coffee, tea and pop for the kids plus cakes, biscuits and buns for afters and the locally produced ice cream which comes in an assortment of colours and flavours. Open all the year round from Monday to Saturday Muffins does not serve hot food after half past four. Bright, cheerful and very good value, this little café is a find. When our selected refreshment stop closes on Sundays, it is nice to be able to offer our readers a couple of alternatives.

The Feathers is a Courage pub set back from the road near Coleford's centre. Food is available and it is reasonably priced and good.

The Angel Hotel over the way, is an old coaching inn whose black and white building offers the usual pub fare plus the atmosphere of a really interesting old building. Both pubs are comfortable and well managed.

Return

Return to the clock tower, memorial cross and Victorian water trough, and continue up High Street then left into the public carpark. Follow the signed cycleway which takes the route of the disused railway track passing the remaining Goods Station. At present this is being converted into a railway museum which plans to open in 1988. An old fashioned booking and ticket office will be featured and railway memorabilia, including the static wagon outside, will be on display.

The cycleway continues between a pump factory and a golf course which is reached by a stile on the left. Please be careful of the golfers who also wish to share the enjoyment of the countryside. Keep to the

71

path bearing right to a line of telegraph poles which are followed to the left passing Lower Edenwall Farm to reach a stile leading onto the Coalway road. Turn right here to the Coalway crossroads, then keep ahead taking the first left turn signed 'Parkend Walk'. Pass a former inn now called Albion House and a small oak grove on the left before returning to the forest.

A forestry track leads past the entrance to the Management Training Centre, and within the next thirty yards bear left by a magnificent copper beech, where a delightful path penetrates into larch and spruce plantations. Upon meeting a main track, turn right to eventually reach a pair of gates, turn sharp left here through the first one to follow a track gently descending towards the Cannop valley. Enter enclosed woodland on the left by a stile, then turn immediately to the right along a narrower path going steeply down the wooded slope. Known locally as the Miner's Path this is the quickest route from Coalway to Cannop.

On reaching the bottom a main track leads left then right to the road opposite the Forest of Dean Stone Firms, which over the last two hundred years have cut and shaped the sandstone blocks quarried from Bixslade. Turn left past these stone works to arrive at the lower end of Cannop Ponds. From here rejoin the waymarked path leading across a wooden bridge and along the right hand side of the ponds back to the carpark.

4 miles

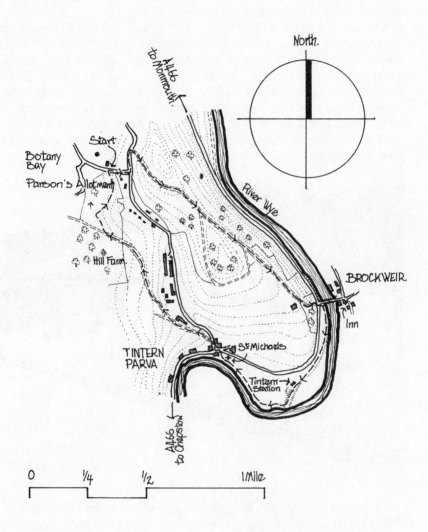

Located in south east Wales, Tintern is nationally renowned, thanks to William Wordsworth, for its Cistercian Abbey founded in 1131 on the banks of the Wye. Now a Welsh Historic Monument the romantic roofless ruins are open to the public all the year round. Within half a mile lies the more recent remains of the Wye Valley Railway which operated from 1876 to 1964.

The former station, platform, signal box and railway track at Tintern have been cleverly restored and converted by the Wye Valley Wardens and the Gwent County Council into an excellent picnic site, information centre and refreshment room. Static railway coaches contain a well documented exhibition of the Wye Valley Railway and past local industries. Pre-booked school parties are particularly welcome. Three short waymarked walks lead along the old railway track, beside the Wye and across the river to Brockweir and Caswell Wood.

Tintern Station.

Our short energetic four mile ramble starts from the slopes of Botany Bay beside the busy Cat Brook, before steeply descending from the Forestry Commissions's woods at Coed Beddick following the route of the Wye Valley Walk. This long distance path extends from Chepstow through the market towns of Monmouth and Ross-on-Wye to the cathedral city of Hereford, a distance of some fifty miles. It is clearly waymarked with yellow arrows and provides a beautiful and varied route through the scenic Wye Valley. Shortly after Tintern Station leave the marked path and return along an uphill route comprising ancient paths and functional forest tracks.

Route
This straightforward ramble starts from a small parking area at Parson's Allotment (GR 526020) near Botany Bay in the Lower Wye Valley. Facing Honeysuckle Cottage turn right down a tarmaced lane where a herd of pigs happily root and mud bathe beside the tumbling Cat Brook. At the T-junction turn left along the road to Trellech leading through a steep sided valley with cottages attractively dotted amongst the trees. Within 200 yards, just before a modern white washed house with a red tiled roof, follow the Wye Valley Walk waymarks to the right through the thickly wooded Coed Beddick.

These woods are managed by the Forestry Commission whose policy is to make them an accessible attraction to the public, as well as producing a cash crop from the timber. Muddy in winter and churned to a thick paste by heavy forestry vehicles this rutted track passes a mixture of oak, holly and beech above the brambles and bracken before ascending to a clump of conifers on the left hand side. Here the route forks to the left along an easier path leading to a barrier clearly marked with yellow Wye Valley Walk arrows. The path narrows, skirting a larch plantation on the left; glimpses of the Wye and white washed cottages below at Brockweir will be seen through the trees. Yellow arrows direct the route around a stone wall before steeply zig zagging down to the Tintern road.

Cross the road and if you cannot resist the temptations of the Brockweir Inn, and the delights of this Gloucestershire village then walk over the iron bridge. Built in 1906 it was restored last year by the Gwent and Gloucestershire County Councils. Remains of the old quays can still be identified on the river bank, where in earlier days supplies were loaded and unloaded from the sailing barges, known locally as trows. Nowadays Brockweir is a quiet place, where an atmosphere of the past lingers amongst attractive buildings grouped close to the river. Apart from a pub Brockweir has a village store, pottery and an unusual Moravian Chapel founded in 1831. It is also on Offa's Dyke Path.

If by-passing the attractions of Brockweir then continue along the Wye Valley Walk leading over a stile on the right of the approach to the bridge. Follow the disused railway track which leads straight to the Tintern Picnic Site. Between the trees there is a good view over the Wye of Brockweir Chapel and open fields below thick woods.

Refreshment

Tintern Station is irresistibly set in romantic steam railway land. The old refurbished station is used as a buffet, but nowhere is there a suggestion of curling British Rail sandwiches. Decorated with railway notices, models and plaques it has the atmosphere of a real period Great Western Railway country station. How delightful it must have been in its heyday with the Wye flowing peacefully nearby and tree lined hills rising to the skyline.

A signal box provides an area for browsing among guide books and tourist information, and three old carriages are used for display purposes. Young children can amuse themselves in the rustic play ground while their elders may choose to cook on the open barbeque pits. During the opening season, from April 1st through to the end of October, the refreshment room is managed by a pleasant local couple who sell homemade sandwiches, cakes, pastries, sweets, crisps, tea, coffee, ice cream and soft drinks. The tables are set on quarry tiled floors and if weather permits walkers may sit outside and eat their food amid the most peaceful scene imaginable. A good alternative before arriving at the Railway Station is found over the bridge at Brockweir.

The Brockweir Inn is a friendly little two bar pub with a good coal fire, offering a reasonable opportunity for a hot snack with a glass of Hook Norton real ale.

Return

After refreshments, continue following the Wye Valley Walk along the railway track to the river, then turn right down the embankment and follow the banks of the Wye as directed by the waymarks. Now in open fields the scenery improves, ancient hawthorns clad with ivy, steep wooded slopes of distant misty hills and a recently planted vineyard on a south facing slope. The river Wye's unpolluted waters are famous for salmon fishing, and the whole river provides a quiet setting for wildlife. Grey wagtail and common sandpiper are frequently found in fast stretches. Kingfishers use the shallow pools and moorhen and coot are commonly seen along the slower stretches. During summer the riverside is covered with a rich variety of wild flowers including the tall pink Himalayan Balsam.

76

A stone stile leads into the graveyard of St. Michael's church at Tintern Parva. The small restored stone building with its tiny bell turret is surrounded by thick old yew trees, indicating an ancient site which belonged to the abbots of Tintern. Leave the churchyard where yellow arrows lead along a stone walled lane to the main road. Here the Wye Valley Walk goes left on its way to Chepstow, but our route crosses the road to follow the turn ahead to Catsbrook. After about 100 yards turn left by Bankside following an ancient rock strewn lane climbing steeply to forestry plantations. Drifting aroma of wood smoke is evocative as one climbs this sunken byway lined with stones and dried rusty bracken.

A letter box clearly signed Hill Cottage is passed before reaching a white gate, where our rocky path bears left in front of a renovated cottage. During winter a series of spring-fed streams flow across the path whose high moss-covered stone walls are shaded by ivy, fern, holly, beech and birch. At the top a gate on the right makes a good viewpoint of the river below the wooded and bracken clad hills of the Wye Valley.

From this gate follow the left hand fork where our path's stone wall is replaced by gnarled and knotted old beech hedges. At last the Forestry Commission's woods are reached. Keep ahead along a wide track and at the next T-junction turn right to follow a track which meanders pleasantly back to Parson's Allotment.

BIBLIOGRAPHY

Richard Shegog, Symonds Yat Official Guide, 1984
Herefordshire and Radnorshire Nature Trust, Nature Reserves
Herefordshire Countryside Treasures, 1981
Bob Cross, Industrial Wyedean, 1982
What's On in Wyedean, July 1986
Michael Mountney, Saints of Herefordshire, 1976
Nikolaus Pevsner, Buildings of Herefordshire, 1963
Herefordshire Directories, 1858 and 1902
Mary Andere, Homes and Houses, 1977
S.D. Coates and D.G. Tucker, Water Mills, 1983
Dept. of Environment, Skenfrith Castle, 1970
St. Bridget's Church Guide
Mary Hopson, Burial Ground at Coed Anghred
Bygone Days in the March Wall of Wales, 1926
J.A. Bradney, History of Monmouthshire, 1904
E. Jervoise, Ancient Bridges of Wales, 1936
British Waterways, Monmouthshire and Brecon Canal
A.D. Muir, History and Guide of Llangattock, 1982
Church of Saint Mary Magdalene, 1978
J.W. Tonkin, Herefordshire, 1977
Kington Town Guide
Literary Kington
Knighton Guide
National Trust, Berrington Hall
Medieval Site at Breinton, Trans. of Woolhope Club, Vol. 38, 1963
Forestry Commission, Boy's Grave and Cannop Forest Trail, 1974
Coleford, Forest Town Guide
Wyedean Tourist Board, Royal Forest of Dean Guide
Lower Wye Valley Preservation Society, Miscellany, 1977
H.W. Parr, An Industrial Tour, 1980
Tintern Station Picnic Area Guide. History of St. Faith's Church, 1985
Ian Wraight and Mark Dyer, Real Ale in Herefordshire, 1980
Trevor Rowley, Welsh Marches, 1986
Keith Kissack, The River Wye, 1978
Countryside Commission, Out in the Country, 1985

USEFUL ADDRESSES

Countryside Commission, John Dower House, Crescent Place,
  Cheltenham, Glos.
Herefordshire and Radnorshire Nature Trust, 25 Castle Street,
  Hereford
Ramblers' Association, 1/5 Wandsworth Road, London, SW8
  2XX
Hereford and Worcester County Council, County Hall,
  Spetchley Road, Worcs.
Gwent County Council, County Hall, Cwmbran, Gwent
Gloucestershire County Council, Shirehall, Gloucester
Powys County Council, County Hall, Llandrindod Wells, Powys
Wye Valley Countryside Service, Hadnock Road Depot,
  Hadnock Road, Monmouth
Coleford Tourist Information Centre, Market Place, Coleford,
  Glos.
Wyedean Tourist Board, 20 Broad Street, Ross-on-Wye,
  Herefordshire
Monmouth Tourist Information Centre, Church Street,
  Monmouth, Gwent
Forestry Commission, Crown Office, Coleford, Gloucestershire
National Trust, 36 Queen Anne's Gate, London SW1H 9AS
Offa's Dyke Association, Old Primary School, Knighton, Powys
Ross-on-Wye Civic Society, Right of Way Committee, The Sec.
  2 Woodside, Welsh Newton, Monmouth
English Heritage, PO Box 43, Ruislip, Middx.
Welsh Historic Monuments, Brunel House, 2 Fitzalan Road,
  Cardiff
Country Landowners' Association, 16 Belgrave Square, London
  SW1X 8PQ
Open Spaces Society, 25a Bell Street, Henley on Thames, Oxon
Ordnance Survey, Romsey Road, Maybush, Southampton,
  Hants
Royal Society for the Protection of Birds, The Lodge, Sandy,
  Beds.

THE AUTHORS

Heather Hurley as a Voluntary Countryside Warden and Chairman of the Ross Civic Society Rights of Way Committee has first hand experience of the problems of keeping the miles of rights of way open and in use by the general public. She is the author of several publications on local history and walking including 'Wyedean Walks', and has personally researched and written walks for twelve years. Her other hobbies include riding, local history and gardening.

Jon Hurley lectures, writes and broadcasts on the subject of wine, and his book 'Wines with Game and Fish' was published last year. He has also written two popular guides to the pubs of Herefordshire and the Forest of Dean and a collection of poems entitled 'The Wicked Wind'. He enjoys walking, golf, foreign travel, food and like Heather takes a keen interest in gardening and the countryside.

Their first joint venture 'Paths and Pubs of the Wye Valley' published by Thornhill Press was critically well received and continues to be a popular seller.